GROWING UP UNTO THE LORD

I LOVE THIS BOOK! HAVE YOU EVER wanted to see behind the scenes in a great leader's life? Elder Cardon takes us there. In this wonderful book he shares moving personal experiences from his youth, courtship, and parenting. He imparts valuable insights learned over a lifetime of gospel study and service. With the gentleness of a loving father and grandfather, he teaches us that growing up unto the Lord is much more than getting older and, in his own words, "Conversion is much more than compliance. . . . The difference is always in the heart." This book points us to the Lord and offers simple and practical ways to get His gospel into our hearts and the hearts of those we most love.

—BRAD WILCOX, BYU PROFESSOR OF ANCIENT SCRIPTURE
AND AUTHOR OF *The Continuous Atonement*

CRAIG CARDON SHARES HIS HEARTFELT INSIGHTS AND real-life experiences as he masterfully uses the scriptures to teach how he learned to receive, recognize, and respond to the voice of the Lord in his personal life and how he has applied these truths in his family and in his service to others. This book is a treasure to parents and leaders of youth but also to anyone who desires to have the constant guiding and comforting presence of the Holy Ghost in their lives. The doctrine and principles he teaches are clear and simple, and his personal stories help the reader see how these truths can be applied in our lives on a daily basis to guide not only our personal decisions but also our actions and reactions. As I associated with Craig Cardon in my former calling as General Young Women president for The Church of Jesus Christ of Latter-day Saints, I observed a man who has become familiar with the voice of the Lord through his faithful, covenant-keeping life. I learned deeply from him as we counseled together and have been hoping he would share his insights and experiences with all in written form. Once again, he has responded to the promptings of the Spirit in sharing his sacred personal insights with us. I, for one, am grateful for this little gem and highly recommend its contents and truths to anyone who desires to grow in spirit.

—ELAINE DALTON

IN A WORLD WHERE WE ARE ALL concerned about how to help our children and grandchildren navigate through these difficult times I believe that *Growing Up Unto the Lord: Recognizing and Responding to the Voice of the Spirit, Living in Peace, and Blessing Generations* by Craig A. Cardon provides insight on how to help these precious young people. I have known Craig and Debbie Cardon since 2006. I have seen that they practice what they preach. A few years ago, I attended a meeting where Craig said, "Debbie and I were not perfect in the rearing of our eight children—far from it. Nonetheless, with the birth of our first child nearly fifty years ago, we began praying daily, individually and unitedly, that our children would develop the capacity to recognize the voice of the Spirit and would have the courage to respond to the Lord's counsel and direction. These daily prayers have never ceased and continue today and now include our grandchildren and great grandchildren." I have used this quote countless times.

This book is enlightening with sound doctrine, principles, and how to's. As I read, I was inspired and found great truths that will help all of us. I wish that Mary Anne and I had this book when we were young parents. We will buy one for all of our children, grandchildren, and special friends. Following the great truths contained in this book will bless and help generations. Thank you, Craig, for writing this book.

—DON CLARKE

GROWING UP UNTO THE LORD

GROWING UP UNTO THE LORD

RECOGNIZING AND RESPONDING TO THE VOICE OF THE SPIRIT, LIVING IN PEACE, AND BLESSING GENERATIONS

CRAIG A. CARDON

CFI
An Imprint of Cedar Fort, Inc.
Springville, Utah

ISBN 13: 978-1-4621-3866-1

Published by CFI, an imprint of Cedar Fort, Inc.
2373 W. 700 S., Springville, UT, 84663
Distributed by Cedar Fort, Inc., www.cedarfort.com

LIBRARY OF CONGRESS CONTROL NUMBER: 2020950083

Cover design by Courtney Proby
Cover design © 2021 Cedar Fort, Inc.

Printed in the United States of America

10 9 8 7 6 5 4 3 2 1

Printed on acid-free paper

To Debbie: my love, my eternal companion.

CONTENTS

ACKNOWLEDGMENTS

I WILL BE ETERNALLY GRATEFUL FOR MY parents, Wilford Pratt Cardon and Vilate Allen Cardon, who taught me the gospel of Jesus Christ and fostered within my heart a love for Him and a deep and abiding faith in Him and His Atonement. They helped me find joy in loving and worshiping Heavenly Father in the name of His Son and in recognizing and responding to the promptings of the Holy Ghost in seeking truth, comfort, strength, protection, and direction. They also taught me to hearken to the voice of the Lord by hearkening to the teachings of His living prophets.

My eternal companion, Debbie, has done more to refine my nature than any other person in my life. Her charity, patience, faith, and purity have been a constant influence for good in my life since first meeting her in 1965. Her influence continues to refine and teach me.

It is likely that this book would not exist but for the loving assistance of our oldest child, Patricia. Tricia has with patience, kindness, and skillful insights assisted in the editing and refinement of the book through weekly visits over more than a year. And, in their own way, each of the children has contributed to this book through their love and discipleship of the Lord. They are Thomas and Patricia Burton, Aaron and Melissa Petersen, Craig and Aimee Cardon, Andrew and Ann Cardon, Nathan and Andrea Andersen, Daniel and Louise LeSueur, Paul and Raeanna Cardon, and Russell and Malorie Cardon. They and their children, my grandchildren and great-grandchildren, are precious, dear souls and I love them.

Many friends and associates have also contributed to this book with their invaluable teachings, counsels, and examples over the years. Brad Wilcox and Don Clarke were particularly helpful in their reviews of the manuscript.

Finally, I desire to make it clear that I am solely responsible for the opinions and views expressed in this book and for any errors that may be present herein. This book has not been written under assignment of or at the request of the First Presidency or the Quorum of the Twelve Apostles and is not a Church publication. Therefore, the views expressed in this book do not represent the official position of The Church of Jesus Christ of Latter-day Saints.

INTRODUCTION

WHILE RAISING OUR FAMILY OF EIGHT CHILDREN, the Lord taught Debbie and me some valuable lessons. I remember how amazed I was when looking upon our first child, a daughter. I felt the love within my heart expand in ways I had not anticipated and found difficult to describe. That experience was repeated as love expanded with the addition of each precious soul to our family. It seems simple to say, but the Lord taught me within the depth of my being that love grows; it is not merely divided.

We also learned how willing the Lord is to bless, direct, encourage, and sustain neophyte parents as they seek to rear children in righteousness. Beyond the possibly programmatic aspects of gospel living within a home, such as daily scripture reading, prayer, weekly worship, and renewal of covenants and family home evening, we received remarkable spiritual guidance according to individual needs and circumstances as we sought help on unique developments over the years in the lives of these precious children. Beyond the necessary and helpful programmatic practices, these were heart-changing experiences often effectuated through small means that could have been easily missed. Nonetheless, acknowledging our weakness and imperfection as parents, we found the Lord patient and willing to assist. In seeking His help, we learned that we had to be attentive to see the teaching moments He presented, and to not miss or ignore them but to act in faith on them in the moment.

I was called as a General Authority Seventy in April 2006 and was released and became a General Authority Emeritus in October 2018. I served the first five years in the Africa West Area presidency, the next five years in the Priesthood and Family Department, along with a few other assignments at Church Headquarters, including editor of Church magazines, and the final two years in the Pacific Area presidency. While at Headquarters from 2011 to 2016, by virtue of assignments from the First Presidency and the Twelve, I was privileged to witness from a front-row seat the revelatory processes by which the prophets prepared and brought forth the recently implemented initiatives such as the adjustments to priesthood quorums, brother and sister ministers, the home-centered and Church-supported "Come, Follow Me" curriculum, and children and youth activities.

I observed that a primary objective of the prophets is to foster deeper conversion to the gospel of Jesus Christ and a firmer faith in the Lord Jesus Christ and His Atonement. There was a clear recognition that such conversion and exercise of faith come only by the ministry of the Holy Ghost, and that the home is the best place for the influence of the Holy Ghost to be fostered. Under the direction of the prophets, the Spirit of the Lord brooded over everyone involved in conceptualizing, developing, refining, and bringing forth these adjustments and initiatives.

Over my years of service with many weekend stake conference and other assignments, I occasionally felt impressed to address in my teaching the importance of helping all of God's children to recognize and respond to the voice of the Spirit, knowing this topic to be the enduring source and means of deep conversion and the exercise of faith in Jesus Christ. While participating in the development of the new Church curriculum at Headquarters, I began to feel a greater urgency with the topic and began to address it more regularly in my weekend assignments. In doing so, I found that in addition to drawing lessons and examples from the scriptures, sharing my wife's and my experiences in rearing our family seemed to be particularly meaningful in communicating the message. This was evidenced by regular requests from members following conferences for copies of anything I might have written on the subject, but I had written nothing at the time. Several of my brethren of the Seventy also suggested I share some of these things in writing. Near the end of my service as a General Authority, while I was assigned to the Pacific Area presidency, Elaine Dalton, former Young Women General President, visited Auckland, New Zealand, while participating with others in activities encouraging and supporting the women of the Church. In a quiet reception with the area presidency and those with whom she was traveling, she initiated a discussion on some of these principles that I had shared with her and others while serving together earlier and was politely insistent that I write a book. These separate suggestions to write about these things seemed to have a cumulative effect near the conclusion of my service.

Following my release, I felt it was time to put some of what the Lord had taught me in writing, at least for the benefit of my family and perhaps a few others. My wife and I had talked about these things with our children over the years, and they were now in all life-cycle stages of rearing their children. At the time of the publication of this writing we have forty-six grandchildren and three great-grandchildren. Although our children had experienced many of the things discussed in the book while growing up in our home, they also voiced desires to have something in writing to which they and their children could occasionally refer. Thus, this book was written. It is written as if to a broader audience, as it may find its way into the hands of a few outside our family. If so, I hope it will be meaningful and useful to them.

For those readers who may not be familiar with the doctrine of The Church of Jesus Christ of Latter-day Saints or with the scriptural cannon of the Church, I note simply that in addition to the Bible, the Church publishes other volumes of scripture that contain the words of prophets of God, ancient and modern, revealed in these last days:

- The Bible
- The Book of Mormon—Another Testament of Jesus Christ
- The Doctrine and Covenants
- The Pearl of Great Price

In this work I quote from all four of these books. I also refer to the Church's teaching that all of the human family are spirit sons and daughters of our loving Heavenly Father, and He will lead us to truth and happiness through the influence of His Spirit.

Some may find my extensive reference to scriptures and scriptural accounts a bit laborious. Hopefully, our family members are accustomed to this from me and will continue to see in this my conviction that the Lord has provided in the scriptures the doctrine, principles, and practices that respond to every challenge we face in our lives today. When combined with the teachings of God's living prophets and through the ministry of the Holy Ghost, we are able to be taught from heaven. If that is not the source of learning for one reading this book, then the writing of the book and the reading of the book are in vain. My prayer is that those reading this book will find their minds enlightened and their hearts opened by the Holy Ghost, beyond the words on the pages.

1

RECEIVING DIRECTION

It was a beautiful summer season in Trieste, Italy, in July 1968. I had arrived in Italy just a few months earlier to begin my two- and one-half-year mission. The mission was new enough that instructions in Italian had not yet begun at what was then the Language Training Mission, or LTM. This meant that for a season, those called to Italy were given an additional six months in the field to aid in learning the language. And while I had made good progress with the language, there was something that for me seemed to overshadow the work.

Her name was Debbie. I had met this faithful, beautiful, selfless daughter of God in high school. Following the counsel of my parents, we had not dated steadily, but we had dated regularly. I had developed deep feelings for her, and I believed she for me, but my service to the Lord at the call of the prophets had always been the priority for both of us. Indeed, when I departed Arizona for my mission in February, we affirmed to each other that while we hoped things would work out for us after the mission, there were no formal or informal commitments between us. This wasn't the time. She was free to date, and I would devote my time to the Lord.

Upon arriving in Italy, unlike other missionary elders who had pictures of their girlfriends back home displayed in the apartment, I kept the picture I had of Debbie in a drawer, only viewing it on preparation day when I would write to her. But this outward practice attempting to show complete devotion to my missionary purpose wasn't really working. Inwardly my heart and mind were often with Debbie. Personally, I felt conflicted and duplicitous. I was not at peace spiritually. I had prayed much about this during my few months in Italy, but the matter had not rested in my heart and mind.

A few weeks earlier I had written to my father, asking for his counsel. Although it's hard to remember such a time, those were the days before instant email and social media communication. Generally, it took two weeks for a letter to make it from Italy to Arizona and another two weeks for a response to make it back.

My father never held what some would consider to be a high Church position, but the flame of the gospel burned brightly in his heart, and he shared it with everyone. While I served in Italy, he served as what was then known as the stake mission president. My mother was a woman of great and abiding faith. Together, they taught me to pray, to obey the Lord's commandments, and to love the Lord and His gospel.

Dad responded to me with a letter dated July 7, 1968. It arrived a couple of weeks after that. His inspired and even prophetic counsel served to connect me with heaven in a way I had not previously imagined possible, notwithstanding my being immersed in the Lord's work at the time. An understanding of the significance in my life of this letter from my father is enhanced by the fact that the Lord called him home unexpectedly six months later at the age of fifty-nine, making the letter one of his last communications to me during his mortal sojourn. The letter is two typewritten pages in length, typed by my mother as my father dictated. As one of the few written communications I had from him before his death, the letter is precious to me.

Dad didn't tell me what to do about Debbie. Instead, he taught me how to get the answer to this important life decision through the gift of the Holy Ghost. I thought I already knew that, but in this momentous occasion, my heart was prepared as never before to receive a witness of spiritual truths taught to me by my father.

Dad drew parallels between what I was facing and what those learning about the restored gospel face. This reference to what I was encountering each day in my missionary activities greatly enhanced my understanding. Decisions about both obeying the Lord's commandments and decisions about serving Him must be made, and as Dad expressed it, "it all boils down to the fact that none of us, and I mean none, can get along without the Holy Ghost as our constant guide and companion."

Dad taught me from the scriptures, making reference to the Doctrine and Covenants[1] and to how the Lord taught Joseph Smith and Oliver Cowdery to receive answers from Him, studying things out in our minds, making decisions as to a course forward, and then seeking confirmation from the Lord, receiving a burning in the bosom or a stupor of thought. Dad made this faith-filled statement: "I do not know the answer to your problem. The Lord is going to give you the answer and no one else." He then shared his personal counsel as informed by the prophets with this introduction: "But here are a few things you might consider before making your decision."

Experiences from his life followed, along with a few observations of things he had witnessed in the lives of others. In all of this counsel, he was connecting me with heaven again and again. He concluded:

> I know from the bottom of my heart that when the time comes for you to make a choice, He will let you know. . . .
>
> Make your mind up as to what you should do, then go again to the Lord to find out whether you are right or wrong. When you know in your heart that your decision is right, then have the courage and strength to carry out your decision.
>
> I love you son, and thrill with your testimony.[2]

This was not the first time my father had taught me about the influence and ministry of the Holy Ghost. For example, when I spoke in sacrament meeting just prior to departing on my mission, I quoted these words of an angel delivered to king Benjamin:

> For the natural man is an enemy to God, and has been from the fall of Adam, and will be, forever and ever, unless he yields to the enticings of the Holy Spirit, and putteth off the natural man and becometh a saint through the Atonement of Christ the Lord, and becometh as a child, submissive, meek, humble, patient, full of love, willing to submit to all things which the Lord seeth fit to inflict upon him, even as a child doth submit to his father.[3]

Following sacrament meeting, my father came up to me, gave me a hug, noted my quoting of this scripture, and told me it was his favorite

---

1. Doctrine and Covenants 8:1–5; 9:8–9.
2. Wilford P. Cardon, letter to author, July 7, 1968.
3. Mosiah 3:19.

scripture, which I had not previously known. Indeed, at his funeral, his well-used and marked scriptures were on display, opened to this verse.

In retrospect, I recognize that there were many occasions when my father and mother did what they could to help me recognize and respond to the voice of the Spirit, and yet it was on this occasion of great personal need and desire that Dad's attempt to again teach me now found meaningful reception. The scriptures teach the value of repeated attention to teaching eternal truths. Consider an eternal principle of teaching embedded in the following verse: "When therefore he was risen from the dead, his disciples remembered that he had said this unto them; and they believed the scripture, and the word which Jesus had said."[4]

During His mortal ministry, on at least ten occasions the Lord taught His disciples of His impending death and resurrection.[5] And yet it was not until they were face-to-face with the actual event that they began to understand what He had taught them. So it was with me. I had heard the teaching and had even felt the influence of the Holy Ghost, but it was now in this moment of personal desire and need that Dad was able to again patiently teach, and I "believed the scripture, and the word which Jesus . . . said."

Imagine the lasting influence of such inspired counsel from my father at such a critical point in my life. And as significant as were these lessons from my earthly father, even more powerful were the lessons that would soon follow from my Heavenly Father.

After receiving Dad's letter, I felt impressed to begin a private, personal fast during which, as our missionary work continued, I poured out my soul to the Lord on bended knee and in my heart and mind as we traveled about doing the work. A personally unsettling but spiritually peaceful thought rested upon me. I was to write to Debbie immediately, explaining that while I still thought the world of her, in order to have my heart fully upon the work of the Lord at this time in my life, I would not be writing weekly, but would write occasionally as I may feel prompted to do. Privately, given our "non-committal" discussions at the time I left on my mission, I realized this could lead to Debbie not being available when

---

4. John 2:22. (See also John 12:16.)
5. Matthew 12:38–41; 16:4,21–23; 17:22–23; 20:17–19; 26:31–32; 27:62–66; Mark 8:31; 9:30–32; 10:32–34; Luke 11:29–32; 9:21–22, 43–45; 18:31–34; 24:3–11; John 2:18–21; 10:17–18; 11:25; 16:16–30; 20:9.

I returned, but the spiritual impressions were clear and were accompanied by a feeling of hope. I wrote the letter before breaking my fast and put the letter in the mail the next day.

The day after mailing the letter to Debbie, I received a letter from one of my closest friends. I was not at all prepared for the message his letter contained. His full purpose in writing was to warn me that Debbie had been seen recently at several Church young single adult activities holding hands with a particular returned missionary, and to counsel that if I wanted to have any chance of Debbie being around when I returned from my mission, I needed to write her immediately and tell her to stop seeing this young man.

This was the complete opposite of what I had just done. I had never before experienced the emotion that I felt in that moment. It was as if my heart was being ripped out of my chest. Why had the Lord done this to me in this way? When I wrote my letter to Debbie, a comforting, confirming spirit of the answer I had received and acted upon had rested on me. I felt I was at a point to receive whatever would eventually happen with Debbie according to the Lord's will and His timing. But the very next day?! I was overcome with sorrow and a feeling of deep, personal loss.

I couldn't believe the timing. My friend's letter had been in the mail for two weeks before arriving the day after I had sent my letter to Debbie. Unfortunately, my sorrow soon began to be replaced with a bit of anger. I penned a letter to Debbie that vented my feelings, and although I felt better, I did not feel the Spirit of the Lord. I set the letter aside and wrote another . . . and another . . . and another. Each of the five or more letters became calmer and kinder. As my heart and mind finally quieted with the last letter, a peace as great as had been my consternation overwhelmed me as the voice of the Spirit was now able to speak to my heart and mind. The Lord spoke to my mind the same words he had given to Oliver through the Prophet Joseph: "Cast your mind on the night that you cried unto me . . . concerning . . . these things. Did I not speak peace to your mind concerning the matter? What greater witness can you have than from God?"[6]

All of the impulsive letters were set aside and never sent. It would take two weeks for my letter to get to Debbie and two weeks for a response to return. During this ensuing month, the Lord taught me much. Mostly,

---

6. Doctrine and Covenants 6:22–23.

He helped me see inside my own heart and to connect more personally and directly with Him. Was it truly my intent to give Him my all during my mission, or was I just creating an elaborate facade? Did I really believe He had spoken to me in providing the words in the letter I had sent to Debbie? Did I truly trust Him? Was I really willing to accept His will, knowing that He loves me and knows what is best, and act as He directs?

Over the course of the month, my faith grew, and as it grew, my questions were answered. I was anxious to receive Debbie's reply but knew that whatever that reply was, the Lord would bless and direct me. Approximately a month later, when I received the letter from Debbie written after she had received my momentous letter, she made no reference to the other young man and little reference to what I had addressed in my letter. Rather, she wrote of work and school events in her life and made a simple expression of also desiring to do the Lord's will.

My heart and mind were now firmly on the Lord's work and the mission He had placed before me. Debbie and I continued to communicate, albeit less frequently, for the remainder of my mission. While it may seem rationally counterintuitive, spiritually we grew closer and closer over the ensuing twenty-six months. Because the Lord and His work were first in my heart and mind, and because I knew He knew it and Debbie knew it, expressions of closeness with Debbie toward the latter part of my mission caused no sense of duplicity.

Upon my return from Italy, I learned that she had ended the relationship with the other young man prior to receiving my letter. She later told me that also before receiving my letter, she had independently felt from the Lord that she was to be available when I returned, although she continued to date. By the conclusion of my mission we had known each other for more than five years. We were married two and one-half months after my return from Italy.

My experience affirmed to me a principle that C. S. Lewis identified: "Put first things first and we get second things thrown in: put second things first and we lose *both* first and second things."[7] This does not mean that the second things will always be what we may have originally desired. But when we put first things first with the Lord, the second things we receive are always what He knows are best for us and will ultimately bring us the greatest joy.

---

7. C. S. Lewis, letter to Dom Bede Griffiths, April 23, 1951.

Following our marriage, the Lord taught me another important and related lesson about priorities. It was now a new season of life, and I was equally yoked with an eternal companion with the Lord as our Partner. As I pondered on these things, one day in my scripture study He brought to my attention that there are two things in this life He has commanded that we are to love with all our hearts: Him[8] and our spouse.[9] So long as we do the will of the Lord, we love both "with all our hearts" without duplicity.

I also learned a companion truth, found in the similarity of the Lord's scriptural instructions for "love" and "cleave." For greater understanding, it is helpful to note that the word "cleave" is a contranym, meaning that depending on the context of its use, the same spelling and pronunciation of the word can have an opposite meaning. To cleave in one instance means "to adhere closely; stick; cling; and to remain faithful." To cleave also means "to split or divide; to cut off; sever."[10] The use of both meanings is found in scripture. The companion truth similar to love, of course, is found with the first meaning. In all of scripture, there are only two "persons" to whom we are commanded to cleave: God[11] and our spouse.[12] While the scriptures counsel us to cleave or not to cleave unto various "things,"[13] the only persons to whom we are commanded to cleave are God and our spouse, "and none else."[14] God loves us and cleaves unto us as we individually love Him with all our hearts and cleave unto Him. As spouses individually love God with all their hearts and cleave unto Him, and as they love each other with all their hearts and cleave unto each other and none else, all other relationships find their proper divine order as they continue to obey God's laws and keep His commandments.

Although my increased understanding of the significance and power of loving and cleaving as the Lord has commanded provides an example of continued learning, I am not able to adequately communicate the profound effect Dad's timely and inspired communication had on me, not

---

8. Matthew 22:37.
9. Doctrine and Covenants 42:22.
10. dictionary.com/browse/cleave?s=t, accessed September 21, 2019.
11. Doctrine and Covenants 11:19.
12. Doctrine and Covenants 42:22; Genesis 2:24.
13. See: 2 Kings 3:3; Psalm 102:5; Isaiah 14:1 (2 Nephi 24:1); Romans 12:9; Moroni 7:28, 46; Doctrine and Covenants 25:13; 98:11.
14. Doctrine and Covenants 42:22.

only during my mission, but for the remainder of my life in recognizing and responding to the voice of the Spirit. Even now, a half a century after receiving it, I still refer to the letter occasionally and find great peace in knowing that he knew me, he knew the Lord, and he loved me enough to help me better connect with heaven.

At that critical time during my mission, Dad placed squarely on my shoulders the responsibility to seek an answer from God rather than simply telling me what to do. But in the process, he provided guidance, experience, and testimony to help me along the way. He told me he loved me and that he had confidence in me. And perhaps most significantly, Dad's letter—this letter of a father to his son—bore the imprimatur of the Holy Ghost. It was the Holy Ghost who delivered the message, and it touched me to my very soul.

I have relied on this sacred spiritual communication my entire life. I am dependent upon it. Through the precious gift of the Holy Ghost the Lord has guided, comforted, blessed, and protected me in every aspect of my life. I have heard His voice and felt His influence in matters relating to my immediate and my extended family, and in church, business, education, medical, civic, and personal matters. What a gift!

2

PEACE IN TIMES
OF TURMOIL

CONSIDER THE IMMANENT GRAVITY OF THE FAMILIAL, societal, political, and spiritual circumstances during a particularly difficult time in Nephite history. Mormon[1] writes of the repetitive transition of the people from righteousness to unrighteousness and back again from the fortieth year of the reign of the judges to the ninety-first year,[2] a period of approximately fifty years. During the first several years of this period, Mormon records the following significant events.

A man by the name of Pahoran, son of Pahoran, was appointed by the voice of the Nephite people to be chief judge and a governor of the people following his father's death.[3] Paanchi, brother to Pahoran the younger, "was exceedingly wroth" that he was not appointed, began to lead an uprising, "was tried according to the voice of the people, and condemned unto death."[4]

Not long thereafter, Pahoran was murdered as he sat upon the judgment-seat by Kishkumen, the leader of a secret band of Nephites. Kishkumen was in disguise at the time and fled without being captured.[5]

---

1. The Book of Mormon title page; the book of Helaman, heading.
2. Helaman 1:1; 3 Nephi 1:1.
3. Helaman 1:2, 5.
4. Helaman 1:7–8.
5. Helaman 1:9–12.

Pacumeni, another of Pahoran's brothers, was then appointed by the voice of the people to be chief judge and a governor. All of this occurred in the fortieth year of the reign of the judges.[6]

While Pacumeni served during the forty-first year of the reign of the judges, the Lamanites, led by a Nephite dissenter named Coriantumr, boldly invaded the Nephite capital city of Zarahemla, which because of the contentions among the Nephites, had been left under-protected. Pacumeni attempted to flee the invaders but was killed by Coriantumr.

Coriantumr and the Lamanite army he led were eventually defeated by the Nephites, and in the forty-second year of the reign of the judges, Helaman, the son of Helaman, was appointed to fill the judgment-seat, again by the voice of the people.[7]

Around this time a man by the name of Gadianton, "exceedingly expert in many words, and also in his craft, to carry on the secret work of murder and of robbery," became the leader of the band of Kishkumen.[8] Under Gadianton's flattery, Kishkumen went forth to murder Helaman in an attempt to eventually place Gadianton in the judgment-seat. However, in this instance, Kishkumen's plans were discovered by one of Helaman's faithful servants. The servant killed Kishkumen and reported all this to Helaman. When Kishkumen did not return, Gadianton fled with his band into the wilderness, fearing that he should be destroyed. At this point in his abridgment, Mormon makes the editorial observation, "Ye shall see that this Gadianton did prove the overthrow, yea, almost the entire destruction of the people of Nephi."[9]

Mormon goes on to record that in the forty-sixth, forty-seventh, and forty-eighth years there was "much contention and many dissensions," "great contentions, and disturbances, and wars, and dissensions," and "great contention in the land."[10]

Think of it. In the brief period of approximately eight years, the following took place:

---

6. Helaman 1:13.
7. Helaman 2:2.
8. Helaman 2:4.
9. Helaman 2:13.
10. Helaman 3:3, 17, 19.

- The chief judge, the head of government, died.
- His son was appointed as the new chief judge by the voice of the people.
- The brother of the chief judge was tried and executed for treason.
- The chief judge was murdered.
- The murderer remained unknown, protected by co-conspirators.
- Another brother was appointed chief judge.
- An invading army eventually was defeated.
- Another man was appointed chief judge.
- The murderer attempted to kill the new chief judge.
- The murderer was killed by the chief judge's servant.
- The band of co-conspirators fled the capital and perpetrated contentions, dissensions, wars, and disturbances among all the people.

Such wickedness, upheaval, turmoil, and intrigue!

This was the familial, societal, political, and spiritual climate within which Mormon introduces Helaman's sons, Nephi and Lehi. We don't know the ages of Helaman's sons at the time, but around year forty-eight of the reign of the judges, Mormon makes the following profoundly insightful observation concerning Nephi and Lehi: "And they began to grow up unto the Lord."[11] It is hard to imagine in today's world conditions that could be much worse than those of Helaman's time. Certainly, we may consider Mormon's perspective to have direct application in our time.

Grow up unto the Lord

What does it mean to "grow up unto the Lord"? What was Mormon communicating? Surely it includes gaining an understanding of the plan of salvation, the Creation, the Fall, the Atonement of the Lord Jesus Christ, the priesthood, the Book of Mormon and other scriptures, ordinances, covenants, the temple, and prayer. But one cannot fully grow up unto the Lord without receiving the gift of the Holy Ghost and its attendant blessings, for it is through this precious gift that the Lord communicates with us, and it is by this gift that we commune with Him as He sustains us. While one may have an understanding of all gospel truths,

---

11. Helaman 3:21.

without the ability and willingness to hear the voice of the Lord and the conviction to act according to the direction the Lord gives, one cannot fully grow up unto Him.

From his personal experience and from what he was seeing in the Nephite record he was abridging, Mormon identified the means by which we may find peace and prosperity, no matter the surrounding difficulties.

> Thus we may see that the Lord is merciful unto all who will, in the sincerity of their hearts, call upon his holy name. . . .
>
> Yea, we see that whosoever will may lay hold upon the word of God, which is quick and powerful, which shall divide asunder all the cunning and the snares and the wiles of the devil, and lead the man of Christ in a strait and narrow course across that everlasting gulf of misery which is prepared to engulf the wicked—
>
> And land their souls, yea, their immortal souls, at the right hand of God in the kingdom of heaven, to sit down with Abraham, and Isaac, and with Jacob, and with all our holy fathers, to go no more out.[12]

Consider the eternal implications of what Mormon taught. In any age and in any circumstance, "Whosoever will may lay hold upon the word of God." "In the sincerity of their hearts," anyone who is willing to call upon God's holy name may "lay hold," may obtain, the word of God. And how is that word of God received? It comes directly from the Lord to each individual according to circumstance and need, and it comes to all of us through God's true prophets by what they speak, write, exemplify, and direct. But in every instance, it must come to each individual heart through the ministry of the Holy Ghost. In God's plan, each son and each daughter must ultimately lay hold upon the word of God individually through this divine means. Families and groups may give loving support, but ultimately, an individual must "lay hold."

When the more humble part of the people suffered great persecutions and much affliction, Mormon observed, "Nevertheless, they did fast and pray oft, and did wax stronger and stronger in their humility, and firmer and firmer in the faith of Christ, unto the filling their souls with joy and consolation, yea, even to the purifying and the sanctification of their hearts, which sanctification cometh because of their yielding their hearts unto God."[13]

---

12. Helaman 3:27, 29–30.
13. Helaman 3:35

This evidences the value of family and church support, but how is it possible to yield one's heart unto God without knowing personally what it is in one's own heart that is being yielded? And how does one know that but by the communications of the Spirit? Mormon is talking about things that can be known and experienced only if one is able to recognize the voice of the Spirit and has the courage to respond to that voice.

Among all the other things that Nephi and Lehi were being taught in their home, such as an understanding of the plan of salvation, the Atonement of Jesus Christ, and an understanding of covenants and ordinances, they were also learning how to recognize the voice of the Lord and to respond as He directs.

Mormon reports that at this time, wickedness and abominations were among those who professed to belong to the church of God, which resulted from their "making a mock of that which was sacred, denying the spirit of prophecy and of revelation . . . and their boastings in their own strength."[14] He laments, "And because of their iniquity the church had begun to dwindle; and they began to disbelieve in the spirit of prophecy and in the spirit of revelation; and the judgments of God did stare them in the face."[15]

Nephi and Lehi remembered the words of their father, Helaman, "that it is upon the rock of our Redeemer, who is Christ, the Son of God, that ye must build your foundation." With that memory and foundation, they went forth to teach the word of God to the people. And they taught with great power and authority, "for they had power and authority given unto them that they might speak, and they also had what they should speak given unto them."[16]

"They also had what they should speak given unto them." Whatever else can be said of Nephi and Lehi and their having grown up unto the Lord, their capacity to hear God's voice and act upon it was central to that capacity and conviction.

The reality, the significance, the power, of their capacity to hear and faithfully respond to the voice of the Spirit cannot be more clearly represented than in the verses recording what the Lord later told Nephi:

> Blessed art thou, Nephi, for those things which thou hast done; for I have beheld how thou hast with unwearyingness declared the word,

---

14. Helaman 4:11–13.
15. Helaman 4:23.
16. Helaman 5:12, 18.

which I have given unto thee, unto this people. And thou hast not feared them, and hast not sought thine own life, but hast sought my will, and to keep my commandments.

And now, because thou hast done this with such unwearyingness, behold, I will bless thee forever; and I will make thee mighty in word and in deed, in faith and in words; yea, even that all things shall be done unto thee according to thy word, for thou shalt not ask that which is contrary to my will.[17]

If Nephi and Lehi were able to grow up unto the Lord in the midst of such great turmoil and strife, so may we and our children. All of us must come to recognize that voice, with the conviction to always respond according to the Lord's will.

Sober, and quick to observe

Another example of receiving peace and strength in troubling times is found in Mormon's life. Mormon, himself, received the Nephite record, which he eventually abridged, from a man named Ammaron. Ammaron was the great grandson of Nephi, the son of Helaman, and is described in Mormon's abridgment as "being *constrained by the Holy Ghost* [to] hide up the records which were sacred."[18] Mormon explains that "about the time that Ammaron hid up the records unto the Lord," he came to then ten-year-old Mormon and said, "I perceive that thou art a sober child, and art quick to observe."[19]

Sober. Quick to observe. While these words convey qualities that can be understood in a temporal sense, Ammaron was communicating something much more significant to the boy Mormon. As a ten-year-old, Mormon was naturally receptive to spiritual things. Beyond visual observation and communication, Ammaron confirmed to Mormon at a young age that he was developing the means and the capacity of spiritual observation and communication. Ammaron was affirming to Mormon that this spiritual realm is real and can be trusted. This type of affirmation is an essential part of the spiritual development that occurs with all of us. We would do well to be constantly attentive for opportunities to provide such affirmation within our families and within the Church.

17. Helaman 10:4–5
18. 4 Nephi 1:48; emphasis added.
19. Mormon 1:2.

The impact of Ammaron's intervention is evident in Mormon's subsequent description of himself: "And I, being fifteen years of age and being somewhat of a sober mind, therefore I was visited of the Lord, and tasted and knew of the goodness of Jesus."[20]

With these words Mormon evidenced the powerful impact that Ammaron's affirmation had had in his life when he used virtually the same words to describe what he now knew for himself in his adolescent years to be his spiritual nature: "And I did endeavor to preach unto the people, *but my mouth was shut, and I was forbidden that I should preach unto them. . . .* But I did remain among them, *but I was forbidden to preach unto them.*"[21]

Mormon, also living in turbulent times, was now being quick to observe in recognizing and responding to the voice of the Lord. He was evidencing the courage and discipline to respond as he was directed rather than act according to his natural inclinations.

During a portion of my service as a General Authority Seventy, I was assigned to serve in the Priesthood and Family Department at Church Headquarters for five years. This was a remarkably rewarding and fulfilling experience and provided me a front-row seat to the revelatory processes by which the First Presidency and the Twelve direct the affairs of the latter-day kingdom under the direction of the Lord Jesus Christ by the ministry of the Holy Ghost.

I am a personal witness to the revelation received by the prophets for many of the recent changes and adjustments that the Lord has made in the kingdom to foster deeper individual conversion to the Lord Jesus Christ through individual and family gospel learning and living that is home centered and church supported. And the only means of true conversion for each individual heart is through the ministry of the Holy Ghost. In every instance, the adjustments are intended to help each individual and each family better recognize and respond to the voice of the Spirit, in anticipation of all that the Lord has revealed through His prophets that will unfold in the earth prior to His return.

In addition to this personal testimony of the revelatory processes among the prophets and the councils of the Church, my time at Church Headquarters afforded the opportunity to see and feel something from the

---

20. Mormon 1:15.
21. Mormon 1:16–17; emphasis added.

prophets akin to what I see and feel from Mormon as I read his account of the days in which he lived.

I doubt that there is any governing, educational, or deliberative body in all the earth better informed than are the First Presidency and the Twelve on all the challenges, difficulties, and perplexities being faced by the peoples and nations of the earth. While the prophets are informed by many experts in many fields, their travels and personal interactions with people and leaders from every corner of the earth allow the Lord to teach them through the ministry of the Holy Ghost and to direct them in addressing those things of greatest importance and need. But what is most impressive and comforting is that while they know of the familial, societal, political, economic, cultural, physical, and spiritual challenges being faced by God's sons and daughters throughout the earth, they are optimistic, confident, and sure that God lives, that His kingdom is in His hands, and that His people will be blessed, protected, and preserved in the midst of all the turmoil as He has promised.

This does not mean that God's people will be spared the vicissitudes of life. After explaining concerning the coming of the Son of Man, the Prophet Joseph Smith taught,

> It is a false idea that the Saints will escape all the judgments, whilst the wicked suffer; for all flesh is subject to suffer, and "the righteous shall hardly escape" [see D&C 63:34]; still many of the Saints will escape, for the just shall live by faith [see Habakkuk 2:4]; yet many of the righteous shall fall a prey to disease, to pestilence, etc., by reason of the weakness of the flesh, and yet be saved in the Kingdom of God.[22]

Consider the significance and power of President Russell M. Nelson's example of certitude and faith in the Lord Jesus Christ when he shared the following message of hope as a coronavirus pandemic ravaged the world:

> My dear friends, our Heavenly Father and His Son Jesus Christ know us, love us, and are watching over us. Of that we can be certain.
>
> These unique challenges will pass in due time. I remain optimistic for the future. I know the great and marvelous blessings that God has in store for those who love Him and serve Him. I see evidence of His hand in this holy work in so many ways.

---

22. Joseph Smith, *Teachings of Presidents of the Church: Joseph Smith* [2007], 253.

So during these uncertain times, be comforted by this promise from the Savior. He said, "I the Lord am bound when ye do what I say." I promise you that joy is always within the reach of everyone who will hear Him and obey His laws.

I love you. I pray for you. And I promise that you will receive comfort and peace as you continue to hear Him.[23]

This optimism, confidence, and surety are fruits of the Spirit that we may also gain, thereby finding peace and happiness as we follow Him and His prophets.

There is no doubt we live in turbulent times . . . wars and rumors of wars . . . pestilences of every kind . . . the whole earth in commotion—a time of the fulfillment of prophecy. This is the dispensation of the fulness of times. While Satan continues his futile attempts to disrupt the work of the Lord, among the faithful, preparations for the return of the Savior continue. And in the process, peace, protection, understanding, direction, and confidence distill upon us as we recognize and respond to the voice of the Lord. The Savior promised, "Peace I leave with you, my peace I give unto you; not as the world giveth, give I unto you. Let not your heart be troubled, neither let it be afraid."[24]

---

23. Russell M. Nelson, "President Nelson Shares Message of Hope During COVID-19 Outbreak," newsroom.churchofjesuschrist.org/article/president-nelson-message-covid-19
24. John 14:27.

3

HOW DOES ONE HEAR
THE VOICE OF THE LORD?

Sometime during the mid- to late-1970s Elder Rex D. Pinegar of
the Seventy was assigned to preside at our stake conference. As directed
by the prophets, the conference included a stake priesthood leadership
session, and, as was the normal practice in our stake, the session was convened on the Saturday afternoon of the conference. I don't remember the
Church calling I had at the time that would have required my attendance,
but I do remember feeling young and inexperienced. More importantly, I
remember the powerful lesson that the Lord taught me through the ministry of Elder Pinegar during the session. After being called to the Seventy
decades later, I had occasional opportunity to greet Elder Pinegar, who
had since received emeritus status, as he attended general conference ses-
sions. In each meeting, I tried to thank him for the practical perspective
his teachings gave me on a deeply spiritual matter.

While Elder Pinegar was teaching, I remember being impressed with
the thought of how essential it is for the sons and daughters of God to be
able to hear the voice of the Lord so as to be able to receive needed direction from Him in doing His work. A connection was made in my mind
that it is important for bearers of the priesthood to exercise the priesthood as the Lord desires, thus necessitating the essential communication
between God and man in doing God's work.

At one point, Elder Pinegar provided opportunity for questions. I was
seated near the aisle about halfway back in the congregation of brethren and

raised my hand. He called on me, and I stood to ask my question. Although the subject was not new to me, within the context of his teaching I asked if he would share with us his thoughts on how one exercises faith in the Lord Jesus Christ and hears the voice of the Lord, especially in today's world.

He thanked me for my question and asked if I would be willing to assist him in responding to my own question. I, of course, said that I would. He then explained that after a few brief instructions, he was going to ask me to temporarily leave the chapel, go out into the corridor away from the doors, and wait for a few moments to be invited back in. He then held up his scriptures and explained to me that he was going to hide his scriptures somewhere in the chapel after I left, and when I came back in, he would be standing behind the portable blackboard on the stand that he had been using while teaching. Upon reentering the chapel, I was to come up to the podium, approach the blackboard, and without being able to look behind the blackboard, I was simply to ask him where his scriptures were hidden. He explained that he would then, from behind the blackboard, tell me where the scriptures were hidden. I was then to go and retrieve them. He asked if I had any questions. It seemed simple enough, and I had none. He then invited me to leave the chapel and wait.

A few moments later, another priesthood bearer came to the corridor and invited me back into the chapel. I was not at all expecting what greeted me. As I entered the chapel, everyone in the room began attempting to get my attention. Some who knew me were calling me by name; others were just calling out generally. Some were telling me the instructions had changed I didn't need to go to the blackboard. I just needed to sit down and the exercise would be over. Others were telling me that they knew where the scriptures were and pointed to many different places in the chapel, telling me to go there and I would find them. To say the least, there was much confusion and distraction. Although a row of chairs and a modesty wall kept me from seeing underneath the blackboard to determine if someone was standing behind it, the blackboard was there, and remembering Elder Pinegar's instructions, I walked up the aisle and approached the blackboard. As I did so, I gained some confidence as it was now evident that Elder Pinegar was behind the board.

The noise and confusion in the room seemed to grow louder and more intense as I approached the board. With voices all around me, and without seeing him, I told Elder Pinegar that I was there and asked him where he had hidden his scriptures. Because of the noise and confusion, I couldn't hear him well when he spoke. I went closer to the board and said a little louder, "Elder Pinegar, I can't hear you. You need to speak louder." I turned my head and placed my ear very close to the board. I heard Elder Pinegar say, "Just listen closely. If you do, you will hear me well enough." Then, in a calm and gentle voice, he said, "My scriptures are under the chair where I was seated on the stand. Please go and retrieve them." I walked over to his chair, found the scriptures, and lifted them up. As soon as I did, the noise and confusion ceased.

Elder Pinegar returned to the pulpit and helped all of us to draw various lessons from this experience. I cannot say how well others have remembered this teaching, but it had a profound effect on me.

Although Elder Pinegar had used audible communication as the means of teaching, the broader principles impressed upon my heart and mind were the necessity of going to the Source of truth, of being able to discern the voice of the Lord's Spirit in the midst of loud, competing voices, and of being able to actually "hear" the message or counsel that is being given and then acting on it.

This experience was reinforced by a similar teaching given during this same period of time in my life. I was invited to participate in a special, somewhat unique conference bringing together Protestant ministers from around the United States and leaders from The Church of Jesus Christ of Latter-day Saints in an effort to enhance understanding and greater cooperation between the faiths. The conference was conceived and organized by private parties and was convened, as I recall (my memory on the location may not be accurate), on the Westminster College campus in Salt Lake City, Utah. The program lasted several days and included presentations by conference participants and special guests on various doctrinal subjects in attempts to foster understanding. Presentations were scheduled for about one hour with a portion of that time reserved for questions and answers. The presentations were made in a modest amphitheater classroom accommodating about fifty people, with no microphone. The pattern for the presentations generally included a Protestant minister teaching a Protestant view on a particular doctrinal topic, followed by a leader from The Church of Jesus Christ of Latter-day Saints teaching the Church's view on the topic.

Of particular interest was a topic addressing the nature of the Godhead and the role of Jesus Christ. The Protestant presenter was a popular, charismatic, energetic, and engaging minister. He had prepared well and with entertaining and demonstrative forms of teaching, he enthusiastically and gregariously set forth the Protestant doctrine of the Trinity and role of Jesus Christ. His presentation was well received by all, and he received a standing ovation at the conclusion of the session.

Following a brief break, the conference reconvened in the same room. Elder Boyd K. Packer, then a member of the Quorum of the Twelve Apostles, was introduced as the presenter of the Church's teachings on these important subjects. Elder Packer had just arrived and had not been present for the previous presentation.

After being introduced, Elder Packer stepped to the small pulpit that was available to all presenters at the front of the room and began by expressing appreciation for the invitation to speak. In a calm and quiet voice, he reverently introduced his topic and began to teach. Some conference participants were not fully settled in their seats, and there was some movement and commotion in the room. I was seated near the top of the amphitheater on one of the last rows and had to lean forward to better hear what Elder Packer was saying. I noticed others in the room were doing the same. After just a few moments, we were all a bit startled when a minister seated near me on the last row called out with a loud voice, "We can't hear you! You're going to have to speak up!"

With this interruption, Elder Packer stopped, looked up at the man, and with a pleasant expression on his face respectfully responded without changing his volume or tone, "No. You're just going to have to listen more carefully." He paused just a moment and with this invitation, other whispering voices and noises in the room ceased. Then, with the adequate acoustical properties of the amphitheater room, in a normal, quiet speaking voice Elder Packer proceeded. As one of the Lord's Apostles and special witnesses continued, the Spirit filled the room. Elder Packer put forth revealed truth and bore humble, personal witness of the Godhead and more particularly of the Savior's infinite Atonement. We were learning more from what we felt than from what we heard. After Elder Packer concluded with his apostolic witness of the Savior, there was no ovation. There was great peace.

The contrast between the Protestant minister's well-meaning and entertaining presentation and Elder Packer's spiritual witness was quite apparent. And the lesson for me was again clear: If you want to hear the Lord, you need to discern His voice and listen carefully and closely.

But what do we "hear"? What are we listening for? We are anxious to receive divine communications in many different circumstances. How do we hear the voice of the Lord? Please consider thoughtfully the remarkable parallels in the following multi-faceted scriptural experiences recorded over centuries by different people in differing circumstances.

In the early days of the restoration of the gospel, the Lord spoke to Oliver Cowdery on two occasions, providing helpful instruction that benefits us all as we seek to recognize and respond to the voice of the Spirit and as we seek to help others do the same.

After staying with Joseph's family in Manchester and learning of Joseph's experiences, Oliver inquired of the Lord and received a spiritual manifestation that what he had been told was true. He then traveled to Harmony, Pennsylvania, to meet Joseph and shortly thereafter sought a revelation from the Lord through Joseph that would inform him further. In the revelation, the Lord told Oliver:

> Blessed art thou for what thou hast done; for thou hast inquired of me, and behold, as often as thou hast inquired thou hast received instruction of my Spirit. If it had not been so, thou wouldst not have come to the place where thou art at this time.
>
> Behold, thou knowest that thou hast inquired of me and I did enlighten thy mind; and now I tell thee these things that thou mayest know that thou hast been enlightened by the Spirit of truth.[1]

Recognizing when one's mind has been enlightened by the Spirit of truth is an essential element of hearing God's voice. Oliver had inquired, his mind had been enlightened, and he had acted in faith by traveling to Harmony. The Lord was taking this occasion to bring to Oliver's awareness what he had already experienced but may not have fully recognized. By doing this with Oliver and having it recorded and canonized in scripture, the Lord also does it with all of us who read and seek understanding. We ask in faith, we are enlightened, and we act, often not fully recognizing the Lord's hand.

The Lord continued the lesson with Oliver, and with us, by inviting him to think back on the spiritual communication he had received in Manchester: "Cast your mind upon the night that you cried unto me in your heart, that you might know concerning the truth of these things.

---

1. Doctrine and Covenants 6:14–15.

Did I not speak peace to your mind concerning the matter? What greater witness can you have than from God?"[2]

There is a subtle distinction in the Lord's words that is instructive. Oliver had cried unto the Lord in his *heart*. And his answer came when the Lord spoke peace to his *mind*. This is an important pattern in recognizing the voice of the Lord.

The Lord affirms the role of mind and heart in receiving His communications as He instructs Oliver in another revelation promising him that he would receive knowledge as he asked in faith, with an honest heart, believing he would receive:[3]

> Yea, behold, I will tell you in your mind and in your heart, by the Holy Ghost, which shall come upon you and which shall dwell in your heart.
>
> Now, behold, this is the spirit of revelation; behold, this is the spirit by which Moses brought the children of Israel through the Red Sea on dry ground.[4]

The Book of Mormon prophet Enos provides additional insight to the Lord's communication with our minds and our hearts in his account of his remarkable two-way communication with the Lord. Enos describes this experience as "the wrestle which I had before God, before I received a remission of my sins."[5] Mormon provides some perspective to what this "wrestle" entailed when he uses the same term to describe what Alma experienced when seeking the Lord's blessing in behalf of the people of Ammonihah. Mormon writes, "Nevertheless, Alma *labored much in the spirit*, wrestling with God in mighty prayer."[6]

For both Enos and Alma, this wrestling was a spiritual labor during which there was much "back and forth" between them and God to whom they were praying. They were not only expressing themselves. They were receiving God's word as communicated by His voice, the voice of the Spirit. This two-way, positive communication was fostering enlightenment, bringing peace, and confirming truth. Wrestling is not something one does alone, and in these instances, the other party was God as made manifest through the Spirit.

2. Doctrine and Covenants 6:22–23.
3. Doctrine and Covenants 8:1.
4. Doctrine and Covenants 8:2–3.
5. Enos 1:2.
6. Alma 8:10; emphasis added.

For Enos at this time, and for all of us at appropriate times in our individual lives, there was another significant dimension of his hearing the Lord's voice. That dimension was repentance, evidenced by Enos speaking of his spiritual wrestle occurring "before [he] received a remission of [his] sins."

Enos had been taught in the nurture and admonition of the Lord by his father, Jacob. And in a time and circumstance that his father could not have fully anticipated, Enos went hunting alone. In those moments of solitude, he felt his father's teachings, and he described that feeling as being in his heart: "Behold, I went to hunt beasts in the forests; and the words which I had often heard my father speak concerning eternal life, and the joy of the saints, sunk deep into my heart."[7]

This was God, working through the Holy Ghost with one of his sons who was alone and evidencing a willingness to listen. What Enos was "hearing" was a feeling in his heart, occasioned by a memory of things his father had taught him. With this memory and feeling, Enos records, "And my soul hungered; and I kneeled down before my Maker, and I cried unto him in mighty prayer and supplication for mine own soul."[8]

Spiritually, having a sense of guilt for his own imperfections, Enos had been brought to feel the need to know if what his father had taught him concerning eternal life was personally applicable to him, and because of his father's teachings, he knew that God had that answer and would tell him. So he asked in faith. He records the response: "And there came a voice unto me, saying: Enos, thy sins are forgiven thee, and thou shalt be blessed."[9]

What a remarkable response! God's voice declaring forgiveness of sins! And knowing God could not lie, Enos records, "Wherefore, my guilt was swept away."[10] This is an important example for all of us. Having prepared himself, as evidenced by the fact that the righteous teachings of his father had "sunk deep into [his] heart," and with feelings of guilt and unworthiness resulting from his recognition of his imperfections, with earnest desire to know and feel, Enos exercised his faith in the Lord Jesus

---

7. Enos 1:3.
8. Enos 1:4.
9. Enos 1:5.
10. Enos 1:6.

Christ through sincere prayer. And as He had promised, the Savior miraculously forgave Enos of his sins and Enos's guilt was "swept away."

But even as he experienced it, the response elicited a new question and another glorious response. Enos records, "And I said: Lord, how is it done? And he said unto me: Because of thy faith in Christ, whom thou hast never before heard nor seen. . . . Wherefore, go to, thy faith hath made thee whole."[11]

This was no longer a single response to a unitary prayer. This was continuing two-way communication by which God was teaching a precious son who was inquiring with a sincere heart and mind, with real intent on related matters that were developing during the prayer itself as he received divine communication. Because he had exercised faith in the Lord through his repentance and through sincere prayer, with this divine response Enos no longer felt guilt for his imperfections. This was possible precisely because he believed the Savior and knew that it was "through the merits, mercy, and grace of the Holy Messiah"[12] that he was made whole, the Savior having done for him what he could never do for himself.

Bolstered by this revelatory and refining experience, Enos continued to seek God's blessing. He was now prepared to hear the Lord's voice in behalf of others: "Now it came to pass that when I had heard these words I began to feel a desire for the welfare of my brethren, the Nephites; wherefore, I did pour out my whole soul unto God for them."[13]

"I began to feel . . . ." Enos once again described something occurring within his heart. This communication with God had begun with him acting upon feelings within his heart for his own welfare. He had received specific words in response to his pleading. As he had asked concerning the specific message, additional specific words had come to him. Now, a new topic had arisen within his heart: the welfare of his brethren. And as before, he prayed. What he then recorded brings profound added understanding to what he had previously recorded: "And while I was thus struggling in the spirit, behold, *the voice of the Lord came into my mind again saying*: I will visit thy brethren according to their diligence in keeping my commandments."[14]

---

11. Enos 1:7–8.
12. 2 Nephi 2:8.
13. Enos 1:9.
14. Enos 1:10; emphasis added.

Enos heard the voice of the Lord, speaking specific words, giving specific messages. And how was he "hearing" God's voice in this exchange? By words coming into his mind. Having felt impressions in his heart he had gone to the Lord seeking guidance. In response, he heard specific words, specific messages, in his mind. This was not audible communication. This was spirit to spirit communication. Motivated by general impressions within his heart, Enos had inquired of the Lord. The Lord responded to Enos's mind with specific words and messages. Enos had heard the voice of the Lord! And so it may be with us, our families, and all God's children.

The Lord provides additional counsel. With the image of the positive spiritual wrestling of Enos and Alma in our minds, the counsel of Amulek to the apostate Zoramites takes on greater meaning: "And now, my beloved brethren, I desire that ye should remember these things. . . . That ye contend no more against the Holy Ghost, but that ye receive it."[15]

Paul's counsel to the Thessalonians was simple and direct: "Quench not the Spirit."[16]

Jacob, Nephi's brother, asked his people, "Behold, will ye reject these words? Will ye reject the words of the prophets; and will ye reject all the words which have been spoken concerting Christ, after so many have spoken concerning him; and deny the good word of Christ, and the power of God, and the gift of the Holy Ghost, and quench the Holy Spirit, and make a mock of the great plan of redemption, which hath been laid for you?"[17]

Elsewhere in scripture, we are counseled not to resist God's voice,[18] we are given the example of Korihor who put off the Spirit of God,[19] and we are told the consequence of hardening one's heart.[20] We are familiar with Nephi's chastisement of Laman and Lemuel when he told them, "Ye have heard his voice from time to time; and he hath spoken unto you in a still small voice, but ye were past feeling, that ye could not feel his words."[21]

---

15. Alma 34:37–38.
16. 1 Thessalonians 5:19. The footnote to "quench" suggests the Greek word translated as "quench" could also be translated as "extinguish, hinder, suppress."
17. Jacob 6:8.
18. Doctrine and Covenants 108:2; Alma 30:46; Alma 32:28; Acts 7:51.
19. Alma 30:42.
20. Helaman 7:18.
21. 1 Nephi 17:45. (See also Moroni 9:20; Ephesians 4:19.)

As dual beings, comprised of a physical body and a spiritual body which gives our physical body life,[22] God speaks to us by the Holy Ghost. Again, as the Lord said to Oliver Cowdery through the Prophet Joseph Smith, "I will tell you in your mind and in your heart, by the Holy Ghost, which shall come upon you and which shall dwell in your heart."[23]

It is essential that all of us come to understand and trust this communication, that we quench not the Spirit, and that we contend no more against the Holy Ghost.

The Savior explained, "Howbeit when he, the Spirit of truth, is come, he will guide you into all truth; for he shall not speak of himself; but whatsoever he shall hear, that shall he speak; and he will shew you things to come."[24]

When we listen to the Holy Ghost, we are listening to the voice of the Lord. This truth is at the core of a special invitation from President Nelson as the Church celebrated the 200th anniversary of the First Vision, wherein the Father and the Son appeared to Joseph Smith. President Nelson reminded us that God the Father "personally introduced His Beloved Son, Jesus Christ, with a specific charge to '*hear Him!*'" President Nelson continued, "[Our Father] pleads with us to listen to the voice of Jesus Christ, whom the Father anointed and appointed as our Mediator, Savior, and Redeemer. . . . I invite you to think deeply and often about this key question: How do *you* hear Him? I also invite you to take steps to hear Him better and more often.[25]

Accepting and acting on this loving invitation brings us greater peace and joy in this life and leads us to life eternal.

---

22. Doctrine and Covenants 88:15.

23. Doctrine and Covenants 8:2.

24. John 16:13.

25. "President Nelson Invites All to Hear the Voice of the Lord," February 26, 2020, churchofjesuschrist.org/media-library/video/2020–02–1000–hear-him-president-nelson-invites-us-to-hear-the-voice-of-the-lord?category=topics/revelation&lang=eng

4

IS THIS SPIRITUAL COMMUNICATION FROM GOD?

IN THEIR DIVINE ROLE OF "BUILDING UP the Church and regulating all the affairs of the same in all nations,"[1] Seventies are provided with many opportunities to teach, counsel, encourage, and edify in both formal and informal settings. Many of these formal opportunities come through assignments from the Twelve to participate in stake conferences, mission tours, temple reviews, priesthood leadership conferences, seminars, devotionals, and other special assignments. While not always possible, most of my assignments afforded opportunities for allotting time for question and answer exchanges. All of these occasions were rewarding experiences in which the Spirit of the Lord was able to do much teaching.

Recognizing the essential role of the Spirit in conversion to the gospel of Jesus Christ, prior to a mission tour assignment, I would often ask the mission president to invite the missionaries in the weeks leading up to the tour to study carefully chapter 4 of *Preach My Gospel*: "How Do I Recognize and Understand the Spirit?" and to prepare a three-minute talk on what they had personally learned about recognizing and understanding the Spirit during their time in the mission field. Sometime during each of the mission tour zone conferences, a few of the missionaries would be

---

1. Doctrine and Covenants 107:34.

invited to give the talk they had prepared. However, I would be careful to emphasize that when they spoke, we were not looking for a talk on the Holy Ghost, or a talk on what the scriptures teach about the Holy Ghost. Rather, we were looking to hear from them what they had personally learned while in the mission field about recognizing and understanding the Spirit. They could then reference scriptures that recorded experiences and events similar to their own, bearing witness of the truthfulness of those scriptures that they now "owned" because of what they had personally experienced. This occasionally required them to set aside the talks they had prepared and to share what the Spirit taught them and directed them to say in the moment. Invariably, all of us were blessed and taught by the ministry of the Spirit during these special occasions, made possible by prior preparation, sincere desire, and real intent.

The talks were followed by a question and answer exchange. Almost without exception one of the first questions would be, "How do I know if the thoughts or impressions I am having are from the Lord, or are my own thoughts?" Perhaps no other question better highlights or illustrates the unique personal and individual nature of the ministry of the Holy Ghost. Answers and thoughts relating to this question often involved the sharing of examples of what others had experienced in discerning the voice of the Spirit. Answers also addressed doctrine and principles of the gospel and emphasized the importance of learning through the exercise of faith in the Lord. This means acting upon impressions rather than being paralyzed by them, and then "staying tuned" to receive updates the Lord will give along the way to protect us from error.

With this common question so prevalent on every mind, it was also helpful to refer the missionaries to the comments and table found in chapter 4 of *Preach My Gospel*. The table lists numerous scriptural references to the Spirit, grouping them according to their descriptions of how the influence of the Spirit is evidenced and experienced. Following the table, this powerful quote from President Gordon B. Hinckley is shared:

> President Gordon B. Hinckley read Moroni 7:13, 16–17.
>
> [But behold, that which is of God inviteth and enticeth to do good continually; wherefore, every thing which inviteth and enticeth to do good, and to love God, and to serve him, is inspired of God.]
>
> [For behold, the Spirit of Christ is given to every man, that he may know good from evil; wherefore, I show unto you the way to

judge; for every thing which inviteth to do good, and to persuade to believe in Christ, is sent forth by the power and gift of Christ; wherefore ye may know with a perfect knowledge it is of God.]

[But whatsoever thing persuadeth men to do evil, and believe not in Christ, and deny him, and serve not God, then ye may know with a perfect knowledge it is of the devil; for after this manner doth the devil work, for he persuadeth no man to do good, no, not one; neither do his angels; neither do they who subject themselves unto him.]

[He] then said: "That's the test, when all is said and done. Does it persuade one to do good, to rise, to stand tall, to do the right thing, to be kind, to be generous? Then it is of the Spirit of God. . . .

If it invites to do good, it is of God. If it invites to do evil, it is of the devil. . . . And if you are doing the right thing and if you are living the right way, you will know in your heart what the Spirit is saying to you.

You recognize the promptings of the Spirit by the fruits of the Spirit—that which enlighteneth, that which buildeth up, that which is positive and affirmative and uplifting and leads us to better thoughts and better words and better deeds is of the Spirit of God.[2]

Although there will always be similarities, each individual must learn to recognize and respond to the voice of the Spirit through individual experience with the fruits of the Spirit. Because of this, it is also important to recognize that not all spiritual communications are from God.

Paul taught, "And no marvel; for Satan himself is transformed into an angel of light."[3]

Korihor lamented in writing, "But behold, the devil hath deceived me; for he appeared unto me in the form of an angel. . . . And I have taught his words; and I taught them because they were pleasing unto the carnal mind; and I taught them, even until I had much success, insomuch that I verily believed that they were true."[4]

Jacob taught, "And our spirits must have become like unto him, and we become devils, angels to a devil . . . yea, to that being who beguiled our first parents, who transformeth himself nigh unto an angel of light."[5]

---

2. *Teachings of Gordon B. Hinckley*, 260–61. Quoted in *Preach My Gospel*, 104.
3. 2 Corinthians 11:14.
4. Alma 30:53.
5. 2 Nephi 9:9.

King Benjamin cautioned his people, "Beware lest there shall arise contentions among you, and ye list to obey the evil spirit. . . . There is a wo pronounced on him who listeth to obey that spirit. . . . Ye do withdraw yourselves from the Spirit of the Lord. . . . I say unto you, that the man that doeth this, the same cometh out in open rebellion against God; therefore he listeth to obey the evil spirit, and becometh an enemy to all righteousness."[6]

In the early days of the restoration in this dispensation, with all that the Lord was revealing through the Prophet Joseph, there was much interest in receiving spiritual communications. Hiram Page "professed to be receiving revelations" through a certain stone and several members were deceived thereby.[7] The Lord instructed Oliver Cowdery to tell Hiram, "Those things which he hath written from that stone are not of me and that Satan deceiveth him."[8]

So how can we discern and avoid Satan's deceptions? Doctrine and Covenants 50 was given in response to the Prophet Joseph's "special inquiry" about "manifestations of different spirits abroad in the earth" and "spiritual phenomena" that were being experienced among the members.[9] Among the counsel the Lord gave was the following:

> Therefore, why is it that ye cannot understand and know, that he that receiveth the word by the Spirit of truth receiveth it as it is preached by the Spirit of truth?
>
> Wherefore, he that preacheth and he that receiveth, understand one another, and both are edified and rejoice together.
>
> And that which doth not edify is not of God, and is darkness.[10]

To edify means "to instruct or benefit, especially morally or spiritually; to uplift." The Latin root, *aedificare*, means "to build."[11] This was practical and straightforward counsel. If the communication is of God, it will be preached and received by the Spirit of truth, and both the preacher and the receiver will be built up or edified thereby and rejoice together.

A month later the Lord augmented this counsel as He told the elders of the church, "I will give unto you a pattern in all things, that ye may not

---

6. Mosiah 2:32, 33, 36, 37.
7. Doctrine and Covenants 28, section heading.
8. Doctrine and Covenants 28:11.
9. Doctrine and Covenants 50, section heading.
10. Doctrine and Covenants 50:21–23.
11. dictionary.com/browse/edify

be deceived; for Satan is abroad in the land, and he goeth forth deceiving the nations."[12] This is the pattern:

> Wherefore he that prayeth, whose spirit is contrite, the same is accepted of me if he obey mine ordinances.
>
> He that speaketh, whose spirit is contrite, whose language is meek and edifieth, the same is of God if he obey mine ordinances.
>
> And again, he that trembleth under my power shall be made strong, and shall bring forth fruits of praise and wisdom, according to the revelations and truths which I have given you.
>
> And again, he that is overcome and bringeth not forth fruits, even according to this pattern, is not of me.
>
> Wherefore, by this pattern ye shall know the spirits in all cases under the whole heavens.[13]

The common elements in this divine pattern for determining which spiritual communications are from God are that the individuals who are praying or speaking shall have contrite spirits, that their language shall be meek and shall edify, and they shall obey God's ordinances. Obedience to God's ordinances[14] requires obeying them with real intent and faith in Jesus Christ, which is much more than merely inertly participating in the ordinances. If these divinely declared conditions are met, the prayer or speaker may tremble under God's power, but he or she shall be made strong and shall bring forth fruits of praise and wisdom. And then as an essential, final part of the pattern, what is brought forth shall be (must be) according to (consistent with, complementary to) the revelations and truths given by God through His prophets.

It is simply not possible to separate God and His true prophets. Some try to do this, but God does not and will not allow it. If one criticizes or rejects the words of God's prophets, he or she criticizes or rejects God's words. And as soon as they express their criticism or rejection to others, in any way encouraging them to do the same, they set themselves up as a false prophet to others, including those within their own families who follow them, and together they become

---

12. Doctrine and Covenants 52:14.
13. Doctrine and Covenants 52:15–19.
14. "The ordinances of salvation and exaltation are . . . Baptism[;] Confirmation and gift of the Holy Ghost[;] Conferral of the Melchizedek Priesthood and ordination to an office (for men)[;] Temple endowment[;] Temple sealing[.] (*General Handbook*, section 18.1.)

subject to all the Lord has said concerning false prophets and those they deceive. You simply cannot separate God and His prophets. You can't do it. God does not allow it.

This element of the pattern is extremely important. In essence, the Lord is saying that those who will hear and follow His voice must hear and follow the voice of His servants, that one cannot legitimately claim to be hearing and following the voice of the Lord while rejecting the voice of His prophets.

We are familiar with the oft-referenced words from the Lord's preface to the Doctrine and Covenants: "Whether by mine own voice or by the voice of my servants, it is the same."[15] It is worth noting that the principle is also firmly rooted in the oath and covenant of the priesthood wherein we are commanded, "For you shall live by every word that proceedeth forth from the mouth of God."[16]

The Lord again affirmed the principle a decade later with these words: "And if my people will hearken unto my voice, and unto the voice of my servants whom I have appointed . . . they shall not be moved out of their place. But if they will not hearken to my voice, nor to the voice of these men whom I have appointed, they shall not be blest."[17]

Mormon taught the principle as follows: "And wo be unto him that will not hearken unto the words of Jesus, and also to them whom he hath chosen and sent among them, for whoso receiveth not the words of Jesus and the words of those whom he hath sent receiveth not him, and therefore he will not receive them at the last day."[18]

With all of this in place, God then declares that if one is overcome (spiritually or otherwise) and does not bring forth fruits according to this pattern, he is not of Him.

God concludes this augmented counsel by affirming that by this pattern, the elders shall know the spirits in all cases under the whole heavens. The pattern is quite literally applicable universally.

Just as not all spiritual communications are from God, not all emotional feelings are prompted by God. Elder Boyd K. Packer taught, "The spiritual part of us and the emotional part of us are so closely linked that

---

15. Doctrine and Covenants 1:38.
16. Doctrine and Covenants, 84:33–44.
17. Doctrine and Covenants 124:45–46.
18. 3 Nephi 28: 34.

it is possible to mistake an emotional impulse for something spiritual."[19] An example may be helpful.

While serving as a stake president decades ago, we held a several-day youth conference that was attended by more than six hundred youth and adults from our stake. Workshops, service projects, devotionals, doctrinal discussions, various classes, and games all had been a powerful influence for good. The final session of the conference was a combined testimony meeting, held in a large indoor amphitheater venue. The stake presidency, stake Young Women and Young Men presidencies, and stake youth committee members were seated in the front of the amphitheater. One of the youth leaders conducted the meeting. After an opening hymn and prayer, the youth were invited to come to the podium in the front and to use the microphone in bearing their testimonies. We had allotted about ninety minutes for the meeting.

At about the thirty–minute mark, those of us seated in front could see that many of the youth were beginning to show emotion through tears, both at the pulpit and in the congregation. During the meeting, I had noticed that the testimonies being borne by the youth, rather than focusing on the Father and His plan and on the Savior and His Atonement, were emotionally expressing love and appreciation for friends and leaders. In relatively short order, among not a few, the tears began to grow into sobs, and with the tears and sobs, some of the youth began hugging each other as they moved to and from the pulpit and retook their seats, sometimes attempting to sit together in the same seat. Notwithstanding the emotion, no one was being edified, and the fruits being brought forth were not of "praise and wisdom, according to the revelations and truths" given by God, but the youth were obviously feeling something.

At the conclusion of yet another sobbing expression of emotion, and before another youth approached the pulpit, I quickly stood and with a gentle yet firm voice told all of the youth to get back in their own seats, to sit up straight, to stop their crying, and to give close attention to what I was about to say. I told them that what they were feeling was a counterfeit spirit and that we were in danger of losing the meeting to the influence of the adversary unless this was stopped immediately and corrected. I explained that while we may appropriately speak of friendships and associations between youth and leaders, testimonies are to be of our Heavenly

---

19. Elder Boyd K. Packer, "The Candle of the Lord," *Ensign*, January 1983, 56.

Father, of His Son, our Savior and Redeemer, and of the ways His hand is made manifest in our lives. We spoke of how the Lord communicates with our minds and hearts by the Holy Ghost, which shall dwell in our hearts. However, the adversary, being aware of this, will try to use confusing thoughts and counterfeit feelings to deceive us. I promised them that if they were willing to bear testimony of the Savior, the Lord would bless them during the meeting to recognize and discern the difference between the counterfeit emotions they had been feeling before and the spirit they would feel when pure testimony was being borne.

Every testimony that followed was spirit borne, and the Lord honored the promise that had been given to the youth. Now decades later, many still remember what the Lord taught us all on that precious occasion.

Elder Richard G. Scott opened my understanding to another important aspect of discerning between emotions and the Spirit. While I served in the Africa West Area presidency, he asked to meet with our presidency in his office during the week prior to general conference in 2007. At the time he had "first contact" responsibility among the Twelve for West Africa, and the purpose of the meeting was to help him stay current on matters in the area.

As we were visiting, he said something that for me was profound, yet counter-intuitive, and it struck me so deeply that I immediately began writing exactly what he had said in my notes, not following the continuing conversation. This took several minutes. When I had recorded what he had said the best I could remember it, I mentally rejoined the meeting. At the conclusion of the meeting, I held back as others left his office and discreetly asked if I could have just a moment with him. He graciously invited me to stay. I read to him what I had written, explaining how deeply it had touched me. I asked if what I had written was accurate. He read it and said it was. Recognizing that this was something he had said in a private meeting and wanting to respect all appropriate protocols among the Brethren, I asked if I could quote him when I felt impressed to do so in my teaching. He said that I could. Said Elder Scott, "When you have really strong opinions and feelings about something, it is very hard for the Spirit to get through to you. That is why presidencies and councils are so necessary and effective."[20]

---

20. Elder Richard G. Scott, from private notes of Elder Craig A. Cardon of meeting in Elder Scott's office on March 27, 2007.

Elder Scott was helping us understand that strong opinions and feelings are not necessarily evidences of spiritual direction, and he was inviting us to discern between emotional responses, perhaps governed by selfish motives, and the quiet whisperings of the Spirit whereby private agendas are set aside in deference to the will of the Lord. In marriages, in families, in Church organization presidencies, and in Church councils, there are times when there are differing opinions, and those opinions may have strong emotions attached to them. On these occasions, it is important to not let emotion rule, and to listen carefully to the thoughts and feelings of others. With prayerful continuing consideration, all parties seek to understand the will of the Lord in the matter. When parties revert to expressions of how strongly they feel about their position, they are, in essence, attempting to convince others that their inspiration is more valid than the inspiration of others, when in fact it may not be inspiration at all. This process requires patience on the part of all participants as emotion gives way to the flow of the Spirit. When all parities subject themselves to the quiet whisperings of the Spirit, all eventually feel a discernible spirit of affirmation as decisions are shaped through sincere and respectful discussion, "and all are edified and rejoice together."[21]

Counsel from the Prophet Joseph Smith offers further enlightenment. In addition to recognizing invitations and enticements to do good as being from God, we heighten our sensitivity to "the first intimation of the spirit of revelation . . . when [we] feel pure intelligence flowing into [us]."

> A person may profit by noticing the first intimation of the spirit of revelation; for instance, when you feel pure intelligence flowing into you, it may give you sudden strokes of ideas, so that by noticing it, you may find it fulfilled the same day or soon; . . . those things that were presented unto your minds by the Spirit of God, will come to pass; and thus by learning the Spirit of God and understanding it, you may grow into the principle of revelation, until you become perfect in Christ Jesus. [22]

But do we always get it right, every time? As an additional witness to the principles that President Hinckley taught as noted at the beginning of this chapter, Elder Boyd K. Packer emphasized:

---

21. Doctrine and Covenants 50:22.
22. Joseph Smith, Jr., *History of the Church*, Vol. 3, 381.

The seventh chapter of Moroni in the Book of Mormon tells you how to test spiritual promptings. Read it carefully—over and over.

By trial, and some error, you will learn to heed these promptings.

If ever you receive a prompting to do something that makes you feel uneasy, something you know in your mind to be wrong and contrary to the principles of righteousness, do not respond to it![23]

Through study, prayer, and experience, I have learned that we afford ourselves more opportunity to grow in our capacity to recognize and respond to the voice of the Spirit by not constantly questioning whether what we are thinking or feeling is from God. Rather, as we simply act on our impressions, according to the principles that the prophets have taught us, we rapidly grow in our capacity to heed divine promptings and to set aside others. In other words, stop questioning yourself so much. Use your good judgment consistent with the principles the prophets have taught, act, and stay tuned to the Lord. As you act in faith and continue to listen, God will not let you go too far astray without correcting you. You are His sons and His daughters. He loves you and will speak to you as you seek His guidance.

23. Boyd K. Packer, "Personal Revelation: The Gift, the Test, and the Promise," October 1994 general conference.

5

"THUS FAR" AND
WAYWARD CHILDREN

ONE OF THE MOST ENDURING SCRIPTURAL EXAMPLES of a child remaining faithful in the face of uncertain circumstances and monumental opposition is Nephi, son of Lehi. It is significant that his example comes to us at the beginning of the Book of Mormon, a record prepared and preserved especially for our day.

Within the first pages of this sacred record, Nephi communicates the prophetic calling of his father and notes the societal implications for their family as his father declares what he has seen, read, and heard in heavenly vision. The people mocked Lehi and threatened to kill him. Following the Lord's warning and direction, Nephi describes his family's departure from their home into the wilderness and the resulting familial discord. His older brothers murmured and resisted, but Nephi turned to the Lord and the Lord told him, "Blessed art thou, Nephi, because of thy faith. . . . And inasmuch as ye shall keep my commandments, ye shall prosper."[1] Notwithstanding persistent opposition from his brothers, we then learn that Nephi followed the Lord's direction made known through his father and returned to Jerusalem to the house of Laban, who possessed brass plates containing the words of the prophets and a genealogy of Lehi's forefathers. At the peril of his life and with seemingly overwhelming

---

1. 1 Nephi 2:19–20.

opposition from Laban, by following the voice of the Lord that provided inspiration and direction in the moment, Nephi miraculously obtained the brass plates.

While we appropriately recognize these significant acts of Nephi as demonstrations of his great faith, there is something in what Nephi writes at this point of his record that provides an invaluable insight into his perspective of his standing before the Lord and his attitude in anticipating the balance of his mortal sojourn that lies before him. After recording a rich outpouring of the Spirit confirming the Lord's approval of what he had accomplished while following the words of his prophet-father, Nephi humbly and poignantly inscribes this intermediate assessment of his and his father's progress along the path of discipleship: "Thus far I and my father had kept the commandments wherewith the Lord had commanded us."[2]

"Thus far!" There are powerful lessons embedded in that brief phrase, and the role of the Holy Ghost is central to all of them. Without diminishing the many witnesses of the past, Nephi knew that without vigilance, hearts may stray, and it is only with the precious gift of the Holy Ghost that any of us may hope to faithfully face the trials of life, obey the commandments of God, and "endure to the end"[3] to be saved.

According to our Father's plan, no individual or family is spared the vicissitudes of life uniquely extant to elicit the refinements of perfection in each heart. During my twelve and a half years as a General Authority Seventy, I was assigned to preside at hundreds of Church events in diverse parts of the world where I was able to meet some of the most noble and valiant sons and daughters of God inhabiting the earth. Almost without exception, as I took opportunity to come to know these individuals and their families more intimately, I discovered that along with the great joy that accompanies disciples of Jesus Christ, there were also challenges, heartaches, disappointments, worries, and sorrows, often occasioned simply by "opposition in all things," and sometimes occasioned by poor decisions on the part of other family members or loved ones.

The depth of a parent's sorrow occasioned by wayward children is difficult, if not impossible, to fully fathom. But there is a God in heaven who has experienced the depths of such sorrow, even more, who lovingly

2. 1 Nephi 5:20.
3. 2 Nephi 32:15–16.

provides peace. We are all grateful to our Heavenly Father for the account of Enoch's experience when the city of Enoch, Zion, was taken into heaven.

> And after that Zion was taken up into heaven, Enoch beheld, and lo, the nations of the earth were before him;
>
> . . . and the power of Satan was upon all the face of the earth.
>
> And [Enoch] saw angels descending out of heaven; and he heard a loud voice saying: Wo, wo be unto the inhabitants of the earth.
>
> . . . and [Satan] looked up and laughed, and his angels rejoiced.
>
> And Enoch beheld angels descending out of heaven, bearing testimony of the Father and Son; and the Holy Ghost fell on many, and they were caught up by the powers of heaven into Zion.
>
> And it came to pass that the God of heaven looked upon the residue of the people, and he wept; and Enoch bore record of it, saying: How is it that the heavens weep, and shed forth their tears as the rain upon the mountains?
>
> And Enoch said unto the Lord: How is it that thou canst weep, seeing thou art holy, and from all eternity to all eternity? . . .
>
> The Lord said unto Enoch: Behold these thy brethren; they are the workmanship of mine own hands, and I gave unto them their knowledge, in the day I created them; and in the Garden of Eden, gave I unto man his agency; . . .
>
> Behold, I am God; Man of Holiness is my name; Man of Counsel is my name; and Endless and Eternal is my name, also.
>
> . . . And among all the workmanship of mine hands there has not been so great wickedness as among thy brethren.
>
> But their sins shall be upon the heads of their [faithless and disobedient] fathers; Satan shall be their father, and misery shall be their doom . . . wherefore should not the heavens weep, seeing these shall suffer? . . .
>
> . . . A prison have I prepared for them.
>
> And that which I have chosen hath pled before my face. Wherefore, he suffereth for their sins; inasmuch as they will repent . . . and until that day they shall be in torment;
>
> Wherefore, for this shall the heavens weep, yea, and all the workmanship of mine hands.[4]

Our Father in Heaven knows personally the depth of sorrow felt because of wayward children. In addition to this revealing exchange

---

4. Moses 7: 23–40.

with Enoch, we know that during our premortal existence, our Heavenly Father lost one-third of His spirit children who rejected His plan of happiness and followed after the adversary.[5] If our Father weeps, so may we.

As to our earthly experience, particularly poignant was the expression of one older man, a selfless lifelong servant whose personal ministry has blessed the lives of thousands. In confidential conversation he communicated the following:

> I have six children. At one point in my life, my wife and I sat in the temple with all six of them and their spouses to whom they had been sealed. On that day, had the Lord called me home, I believed he would have said to me, "Well done!" Today, two of the six children are divorced. Another is facing challenges with [personal matters]. Still two others are having serious doubts about their personal testimonies. And what does this mean to me? While I have always understood the first things that are central to the doctrine of Christ, faith in Jesus Christ, repentance, baptism, receiving the gift of the Holy Ghost, and enduring to the end, I am now learning the significance of Peter's invitation to add to these first things some important second things:

> > And besides this, giving all diligence, add to your faith virtue; and to virtue knowledge;
> > And to knowledge temperance; and to temperance patience; and to patience godliness;
> > And to godliness brotherly kindness, and to brotherly kindness charity.
> > For if these things be in you, and abound, they make you that ye shall neither be barren nor unfruitful in the knowledge of our Lord Jesus Christ.
> > But he that lacketh these things is blind, and cannot see afar off, and hath forgotten that he was purged from his old sins.

This good brother continued:

> I never expected to be stretched as I have been stretched, and I now understand the second things identified by Peter in ways I could never have anticipated. I also understand how thoroughly integrated they are in the first things.[6]

---

5. Revelation 12:4; Doctrine and Covenants 29:36.
6. From Craig A. Cardon private journal, October 2, 2018.

In considering the challenges associated with wayward children, it is helpful to more carefully consider important perspectives and lessons provided by Lehi and his response to his familial circumstances. There are lessons here beyond what may appear on the surface.

Lehi was a faithful and devoted servant of the Lord who recognized and responded to the voice of the Spirit. He and his wife taught their children in righteousness. Knowing the hearts of his children and having witnessed the good and the bad consequences of their choices, he and his wife continually labored throughout their lives to teach them and to bless them. After arriving in the promised land and not long before his death, Lehi called his family together, including Zoram, Laban's former servant, to teach, to prophesy, and to bless. This is the prerogative of righteous parents acting under the influence of the Holy Ghost, and even the duty of righteous parents when moved upon or directed by the Holy Ghost.

We learn much from what Lehi said and did as recorded in the first four chapters of 2 Nephi.

Lehi spoke first to Laman, Lemuel, Sam, and the sons of Ishmael (Ishmael had died prior to their arrival in the promised land), telling them that if they would hearken unto the voice of Nephi he would leave his first blessing upon them. But he also told them that if they would not hearken unto Nephi, he (Lehi) would take away his first blessing and give it to Nephi.[7]

Lehi then spoke to Zoram, calling him a true friend unto Nephi, and promising Zoram that his seed would be blessed with Nephi's seed, dwelling in prosperity long upon the face of the new land.[8]

Lehi spoke to Jacob, his "firstborn in the days of [his] tribulation." In a remarkable exercise of priesthood power, Lehi promised Jacob that God would "consecrate [Jacob's] afflictions for [his] gain." As if to provide the doctrinal basis upon which this blessing would be realized, Lehi taught Jacob of the Fall, the Savior's Atonement, and the agency of man.[9]

Lehi then spoke to Joseph, his "last-born . . . born in the wilderness of [Lehi's] afflictions . . . in the days of [Lehi's] greatest sorrow." He taught Joseph his family history and the name he shared with the ancient prophet and prophesied of the common name Joseph would share with

---

7. 2 Nephi 1:28–29.
8. 2 Nephi 1:30–32.
9. 2 Nephi 2.

the latter-day seer whom God would empower to bring forth the records of the house of Joseph.

Lehi had earlier promised Nephi that he would be "favored of the Lord because [he had] not murmured."[10] His blessings upon Nephi are implied in all he communicated to the other family members. All of these blessings, promises, and warnings were given according to the inspired recognition of individual circumstances and needs.

After these powerful teachings, Lehi turned his attention to the next generation, the children of Laman, one of his wayward sons. And while the teachings and blessings that he left with his grandchildren are a powerful example of the influence of grandparents and older people on grandchildren and others in a rising generation, the embedded personal implications for the faithful parents of wayward children, not obvious with a cursory reading, are even more profound. They are lessons beyond what appear on the surface.

First of all, to his grandchildren, Lehi wanted them to hear from his own mouth his oft-repeated promise from the Lord: "Inasmuch as ye shall keep my commandments ye shall prosper in the land; and inasmuch as ye will not keep my commandments ye shall be cut off from my presence."[11] Perhaps Lehi had some doubts about what Laman had taught his children in his home. Regardless, Lehi with great love desired deeply to afford his grandchildren the opportunity to hear the truth and to feel something.

He felt constrained to leave a blessing upon his grandchildren by invoking a promise similar to counsel given in Proverbs[12] that has at times created a degree of consternation within the hearts of faithful parents facing the trials of wayward children. Said Lehi to his grandchildren,

> I cannot go down to my grave save I should leave a blessing upon you; for behold, I know that if ye are brought up in the way ye should go ye will not depart from it. . . .
>
> Wherefore, if ye are cursed, behold, I leave my blessing upon you, that the cursing may be taken from you and be answered upon the heads of your parents.[13]

With an initial reading, one might easily conclude that Lehi, speaking as a grandparent, just confirmed the uncomfortable and unsettling

---

10. 1 Nephi 3:6.
11. 2 Nephi 4:4.
12. Proverbs 22:6.
13. 2 Nephi 4:5–6.

thought often prevalent on the minds of anxious and sorrowing parents of wayward children, that somehow they have failed in teaching their wayward children, and that consequently, whatever "cursing" or consequence may befall their wayward children, no matter its nature, it will ultimately be answered upon their, the parents', heads.

Again, with an initial reading, such an interpretation of the Lord's intent may seem to be bolstered by what the Lord said in this dispensation: "Inasmuch as parents have children in Zion, or in any of her stakes which are organized, that teach them not to understand the doctrine of repentance, faith in Christ the Son of the living God, and of baptism and the gift of the Holy Ghost by the laying on of the hands, when eight years old, the sin be upon the heads of the parents."[14]

However, Lehi is not speaking only as a grandparent to his grandchildren. By extension he is speaking also as a parent to his children. Therefore, what we sometimes miss is that knowing of Laman's waywardness, Lehi just cursed himself with the unique and powerful blessing he placed upon the heads of his grandchildren, *unless* he, Lehi, had taught Laman according to the Lord's command. And knowing that he had taught Laman, he was able with peace and confidence to give Laman's children, his grandchildren, this unique and powerful blessing without bringing a curse upon himself.

Lehi left this same blessing on the heads of the children of Lemuel, another wayward son, with the same implications for himself if he had not taught Lemuel according to the Lord's command.

Notwithstanding the sorrow occasioned by wayward children, with careful consideration of Lehi's experience, a sustained peace can come to the hearts of faithful parents. Lehi had enough confidence in his and Sariah's teaching of their children that he was able to accurately attribute to Laman and Lemuel responsibility for their own choices. And as a loving parent, with Laman and Lemuel no doubt listening to or subsequently becoming aware of his blessing upon their children, Lehi continued to instruct them as to their responsibilities before God for teaching their children. In so doing, Lehi didn't just confirm the powerful truth of parental responsibility for teaching children the ways of God. He brought comfort, peace, and understanding to the hearts and minds of those parents who do this, helping them to understand

---

14. Doctrine and Covenants 68:25.

that while they will feel deep sorrow for their children making errant choices, they may be at peace concerning their own standing before the Lord, for they have taught their children "in the way [they] should go," which "way" includes not only knowing the gospel but also hearing the voice of the Lord. Therefore the children, having reached the age of accountability and having quenched the Spirit, are now accountable before the Lord.

Some members of the Church may question if God really speaks to man because, they say, they have never had spiritual experiences wherein they have heard His voice, or "felt" or "heard" the voice of His Spirit. Laman and Lemuel made such claims. Even after an angel of the Lord had appeared unto them,[15] when Nephi asked them if they had inquired of the Lord on a matter requiring spiritual engagement, Laman and Lemuel's blithe response was a closed heart and a closed mind conclusion: "The Lord maketh no such thing known unto us."[16] Nephi implored them, inviting them to remember these words of the Lord: "If ye will not harden your hearts, and ask me in faith, believing that ye shall receive, with diligence in keeping my commandments, surely these things shall be made known unto you."[17]

The word the Lord used was "surely," according to the conditions He has set. This is not a matter of the Lord not speaking. It is a matter of individuals not hearing. And often, they do not hear because they demand to hear according to their individual terms and conditions, at odds with the Lord's. It is as if they say, "Speak to me at this time and in this way, and then I will hear." And then they claim God does not speak to them when their conditions are not met.

Consider another example from the Book of Mormon. After listening to King Benjamin's address, the people of Zarahemla "all cried with one voice, saying: Yea, we believe all the words which thou hast spoken unto us; and also, we know of their surety and truth, because of the Spirit of the Lord Omnipotent, which has wrought a mighty change in us, or in our hearts, that we have no more disposition to do evil, but to do good continually."[18]

---

15. 1 Nephi 3:29.
16. 1 Nephi 15:8–9.
17. 1 Nephi 15:11.
18. Mosiah 5:2.

This was a powerful, deep, spiritual conversion for all. Indeed, an entire generation was converted unto the Lord. And it was recorded "that there was not one soul, except it were little children, but who had entered into the covenant and had taken upon them the name of Christ."[19]

We understand the reference to "little children" to describe young children who had not yet reached the age of accountability. So, what happened to them? Their parents experienced a deep, spiritual conversion and had covenanted with the Lord, but what happened with the children?

> Now it came to pass that there were many of the rising generation that could not understand the words of king Benjamin, being little children at the time he spake unto his people; and they did not believe the tradition of their fathers.
>
> They did not believe what had been said concerning the resurrection of the dead, neither did they believe concerning the coming of Christ.
>
> And now because of their unbelief they could not understand the word of God; and their hearts were hardened.
>
> And they would not be baptized; neither would they join the church. And they were a separate people as to their faith, and remained so ever after, even in their carnal and sinful state; for they would not call upon the Lord their God.[20]

Notice how the phrase "and their hearts were hardened" is used to describe the lack of receptivity to spiritual communications and eternal truths. It is always a matter of the heart. This is an important insight for parents to monitor and address in individual, unique ways with each child.

As we can see, the passing of faith and conversion from one generation to the next is not automatic. As recorded elsewhere in the Book of Mormon, this lack of conversion among the rising generation not only affected the Nephites. The Lamanites who had been converted to the gospel experienced something similar with their children.

Just a few years after the miraculous event of a day and a night and a day with no darkness being given as a sign confirming among the people in the land of Zarahemla the birth of the Savior, the Gadianton robbers infested the land and "many dissenters of the Nephites"[21] joined them.

---

19. Mosiah 6:2.
20. Mosiah 26:1–4.
21. 3 Nephi 1:27–28.

> And there was also a cause of much sorrow among the Lamanites; for behold, they had many children who did grow up and began to wax strong in years, that they became for themselves, and were led away by some who were Zoramites, by their lyings and their flattering words, to join those Gadianton robbers.
>
> And thus were the Lamanites afflicted also, and began to decrease as to their faith and righteousness, because of the wickedness of the rising generation.[22]

Mormon identifies both the timing and the central cause of sorrow caused by the rising generation among the Lamanites. The description that they "began to wax strong in years" suggests an age range including adolescence and young adulthood. Mormon himself was fifteen years old when he "was visited of the Lord, and tasted and knew of the goodness of Jesus,"[23] and sixteen years old when he "did go forth at the head of an army of the Nephites."[24] With these profound spiritual and temporal elements present in his life at that age, he had a personal sense of when patterns of life begin to take independent form during critical periods of character development. "Began" to wax strong also suggests that Mormon knew that such development occurs over time, and that needed refinements to character were yet possible. In this light, the importance of helping all of our Father's children to gain confidence in their capacity to recognize and respond to the voice of the Spirit cannot be overstated.

As to the cause, "they became for themselves" suggests that those in the rising generation causing the Lamanites sorrow would not receive direction from the Spirit. They were going to follow after their own selfish desires rather than seeking to know and do the will of the Father.

It is instructive to recognize the symmetry in Mormon's language used in distinguishing children who remained faithful and children who fell away. Of faithful Nephi and Lehi, sons of Helaman, he wrote, "They began to grow up unto the Lord."[25] Of the unfaithful Lamanite children he wrote that they "did grow up . . . and . . . became for themselves." How important it is for all of us to help one another grow up unto the Lord!

---

22. 3 Nephi 1:29–30.
23. Mormon 1:15.
24. Mormon 2:1–2.
25. Helaman 3:21.

In His preface to the Doctrine and Covenants, the Lord spoke with clarity concerning the inclination to follow our own will, providing a warning to all:

> And the day cometh that they who will not hear the voice of the Lord, neither the voice of his servants, neither give heed to the words of the prophets and apostles, shall be cut off from among the people;
>
> For they have strayed from mine ordinances, and have broken mine everlasting covenant;
>
> They seek not the Lord to establish his righteousness, but every man walketh in his own way, and after the image of his own god.[26]

While serving as stake president, I counseled with one of the bishops in our stake who, along with quorum leaders, was working with the father in a member family in the ward who would not allow his intelligent, healthy, engaging eight-year-old child to be baptized because he felt that the age of eight was too young for a child to be held accountable for a testimony of Jesus Christ and too young to receive the gift of the Holy Ghost. While the child was eventually baptized at age nine as a "convert," the father had abdicated his divine fatherly role and, at the time, his children suffered accordingly. The family soon moved from the area, and I don't know what happened in subsequent years. Hopefully, the father eventually heeded the counsel of his bishop, his quorum leaders, and the Lord and faithfully fulfilled his divine fatherly role in teaching his children to "understand the doctrine of repentance faith in Christ the Son of the living God, and of baptism and the gift of the Holy Ghost by the laying on of the hands, when eight years old," or, as the Lord says, "The sin be upon the heads of the parents."[27] In any event, the experience provided an example of how easily conversion to the Lord Jesus Christ and familiarity with the workings of the Spirit can be lost to future generations.

But there is always hope. The scriptures teach that because of the Atonement of the Lord Jesus Christ, even the wicked who were destroyed by the flood at the time of Noah will have opportunity to repent.[28]

Consider the oft-repeated statement of Elder Orson F. Whitney wherein he refers to an expression made by Joseph Smith:

---

26. Doctrine and Covenants 1:14–16.
27. Doctrine and Covenants 68:25.
28. Moses 7:38–39; 1 Peter 3:18–20; 4:6.

The Prophet Joseph Smith declared—and he never taught a more comforting doctrine—that the eternal sealings of faithful parents and the divine promises made to them for valiant service in the Cause of Truth, would save not only themselves, but likewise their posterity. Though some of the sheep my wander, the eye of the Shepherd is upon them, and sooner or later they will feel the tentacles of Divine Providence reaching out after them and drawing them back to the fold. Either in this life or the life to come, they will return. They will have to pay their debt to justice; they will suffer for their sins; and may tread a thorny path; but if it leads them at last, like the penitent Prodigal, to a loving and forgiving father's heart and home, the painful experience will not have been in vain. Pray for your careless and disobedient children; hold on to them with your faith. Hope on, trust on, till you see the salvation of God. Who are these straying sheep—these wayward sons and daughters? They are children of the Covenant, heirs to the promise, and have received, if baptized, the Gift of the Holy Ghost, which makes manifest the things of God.[29]

President James E. Faust stated, "I believe and accept [this] comforting statement of Elder Orson F. Whitney." He then shared these additional thoughts:

A principle in this statement that is often overlooked is that they must fully repent and "suffer for their sins" and "pay their debt to justice." I recognize that now is the time "to prepare to meet God" (Alma 34:32). If the repentance of the wayward children does not happen in this life, is it still possible for the cords of the sealing to be strong enough for them yet to work out their repentance? In the Doctrine and Covenants we are told, "The dead who repent will be redeemed, through obedience to the ordinances of the house of God, and after they have paid the penalty of their transgressions, and are washed clean, shall receive a reward according to their works, for they are heirs of salvation" (D&C 138:58–59).

. . . Mercy will not rob justice, and the sealing power of faithful parents will only claim wayward children upon condition of their repentance and Christ's Atonement. Repentant wayward children will enjoy salvation and all the blessings that go with it, but exaltation is much more. It must be fully earned. The question as to who will be exalted must be left to the Lord in His mercy.

President Faust went on to say:

---

29. Orson F. Whitney, Conference Report, April 1929, 110.

Who are good parents? They are those who have lovingly, prayer-fully, and earnestly tried to teach their children by example and precept "to pray, and to walk uprightly before the Lord."[30] This is true even though some of their children are disobedient or worldly. Children come into this world with their own distinct spirits and personality traits. Some children "would challenge any set of parents under any set of circumstances . . . . Perhaps there are others who would bless the lives of, and be a joy to, almost any father or mother."[31] Successful parents are those who have sacrificed and struggled to do the best they can in their own family circumstances.[32]

President Boyd K. Packer provided the following words of comfort:

> The measure of our success as parents . . . will not rest solely on how our children turn out. That judgment would be just only if we could raise our families in a perfectly moral environment, and that now is not possible.
>
> It is not uncommon for responsible parents to lose one of their children, for a time, to influences over which they have no control. They agonize over rebellious sons or daughters. They are puzzled over why they are so helpless when they have tried so hard to do what they should.
>
> It is my conviction that those wicked influences one day will be overruled . . . .
>
> We cannot overemphasize the value of temple marriage, the bind-ing ties of the sealing ordinance, and the standards of worthiness required of them. When parents keep the covenants they have made at the altar of the temple, their children will be forever bound to them.[33]

As we look to teach our children and each other how to be richly blessed by the precious gift of the Holy Ghost and to deepen our con-version to the Lord Jesus Christ, we know that there is no substitute for daily individual and family scripture study and prayer, weekly family home evening, and faithful participation in church meetings and gospel

---

30. Doctrine and Covenants 68:28.
31. Howard W. Hunter, "Parents' Concern for Children," Ensign, November 1983, 65.
32. President James E. Faust, "Dear Are the Sheep That Have Wandered," April Conference 2003.
33. Boyd K. Packer, "Our Moral Environment," *Ensign*, May 1992, p. 68, excerpt printed in *Ensign*, September 2002, p. 11.

ordinances. And in this process, we are learning the importance and significance of the announcement and teachings of the Brethren at the October 2018 general conference concerning the divine responsibility and accountability of parents to teach the gospel of Jesus Christ to their children in their homes. With the development and subsequent implementation of the Sunday meeting schedule, the new integrated curriculum, *Come Follow Me—For Individuals and Families,* and the new children and youth initiative, the Lord has provided inspired means to assist families in fulfilling their divine duties, which are home centered and church supported. As one charged for a season with responsibilities at Church Headquarters that afforded to me the opportunity to witness firsthand the guiding hand of the Lord made manifest through His prophets under the influence of the Holy Ghost, I bear witness that these changes and initiatives are of God.

We believe that God "will yet reveal many great and important things pertaining to the Kingdom of God,"[34] and He has now revealed through His prophets essential patterns for His people to follow in deepening conversion to the Lord Jesus Christ and strengthening individual capacity to recognize and respond to the voice of the Spirit. As the prophets taught, all of this is being done as God prepares the earth for the return of His Son.

The significance and blessings of these inspired adjustments were made even more apparent by emergency medical requirements arising out of the COVID-19 coronavirus pandemic wherein the prophets temporarily suspended the gathering of the Saints in regular Church meetings throughout the world in order to limit the spreading of the contagious and potentially deadly virus. In advance of this imminent threat and the resulting temporary suspensions, the Lord had put in place through His inspired prophets abundant resources and support from the Church for the gospel of Jesus Christ to be taught in the home, thereby fostering deep conversion and the capacity to recognize and respond to the voice of the Lord.

In following the Lord's counsel as taught by His prophets and as confirmed by His Spirit, we lay claim to His promised blessings.

---

34. Articles of Faith 1:9.

6

FOSTERING THE ABILITY TO RECOGNIZE AND RESPOND

DEBBIE AND I WERE NOT PERFECT IN the rearing of our eight children—far from it. Nonetheless, with the birth of our first child nearly fifty years ago, we began praying daily, individually and unitedly, that our children would develop the capacity to recognize the voice of the Spirit and would have the courage to respond to the Lord's counsel and direction. These daily prayers have never ceased and continue today, now including our grandchildren and great-grandchildren. Our continuing prayer is that the Lord will bless our posterity from generation to generation in their important roles as parents in nurturing these important principles in the lives of their precious children. We also pray that He will bless us to recognize opportunities to foster this capacity and courage in the lives of others beyond our family circle.

In answer to these prayers, over the years we learned some things within our home that we believe fostered in our children this capacity and willingness to recognize the voice of the Spirit in their lives and a conviction to faithfully respond to the Lord's direction. Again, while all of us may be far from perfect, from my experiences I have come to know that the Lord provides to us the opportunity for this blessing of capacity, willingness, and conviction to be developed in our individual lives, with the Church providing needed support to families and to individuals lacking family support.

Beyond a pattern of daily religious practice consisting of individual and family prayer and individual and family scripture study firmly rooted in our family culture, we looked for teaching moments when we would be able to reinforce in our children's lives their recognition of the voice of the Spirit and their willingness to act on the direction received. This almost always meant that rather than giving a quick, efficient, authoritarian, parental response to questions or circumstances our children were facing, we invested time and effort in providing parental guidance in helping our children learn how to seek and receive answers from God. There were times when the authoritarian parental response was needed and employed depending on the age and circumstances of each child, but our constant effort was to turn our children to the Lord. A few examples may be helpful. I begin with a general example that in one way or another and at one time or another was applicable in the lives of all of our children.

Notwithstanding demanding and busy life schedules, which included Church responsibilities that usually began early on Sunday mornings, Debbie and I made it a practice for at least one of us, often both, to be up and available until every child returned home from any activity, especially weekend dates, during their adolescent years. In regular family meetings and monthly individual interviews we counseled together and agreed upon appropriate curfews for various activities and circumstances. While we had standard "home by" times, we were always open to discuss exceptions if the children felt the need. Exceptions occasionally rested with both the child and with us as parents, and we would agree to those exceptions, but if a requested exception did not rest with all of us, it was not granted. The key principle for the granting of an exception was that spiritually speaking, the matter would rest with all of us.

These were in the days prior to the omnipresence and extensive use of cell phones, texting, and other means of easy and instant communications. Therefore, on those occasions when a child returned home later than agreed without prior notice, we might begin to worry about their well-being. When they eventually arrived home, we would greet them and let them know we were grateful they were home safely and that we loved them.

Rather than scolding them for disobeying us or disobeying family rules and imposing some type of punishment, we would engage them in a brief discussion, not lasting too long at a late hour. We would begin by saying something like the following:

"Mother and I know that as you were staying out late tonight, the Spirit of the Lord spoke to you. We know that because when we were your age and did something similar, He spoke to us. Our question to you is this: Did you hear Him?"

The child's answer to that question was extremely important, and we listened intently. If the child responded saying, "No, Mom and Dad, I didn't hear anything," we knew that as parents we had some important spiritual work to do. We would tell the child thank you and let them know that beginning immediately, we would be spending time with them to help them hear and respond to that voice. We knew that as parents the Lord had just provided us with an essential insight to our parental responsibilities with that child and generally within our home. That work would involve much of what is being addressed in this book.

However, if the response was something like, "Yes, Mom and Dad, I heard the voice," as it most often was, we would say, "Good. Now help us understand why you responded the way you did."

The explanations varied. Sometimes they had encountered things beyond their control (a flat tire) or circumstances where they had knowingly exercised agency to assist another in need (a medical emergency). As we were able to discuss these rare occurrences, we could see, and helped them to see, their developing capacities to both discern appropriate priorities and to receive "updates" from the Spirit that would bless them throughout the remainder of their lives.

Usually, however, the explanations evidenced a prevalent disposition to suppress divine spiritual communications and to give precedence to the desires of the natural man. "Why did I stay out late? I don't know. I just wanted to." Such a response was an important beginning. It opened to us the opportunity to understand more. Was this child beginning to show a disposition to actively quench the Spirit? Did this evidence a developing rebellious nature? Or was this a son or a daughter of God now in the midst of a divine pattern of spiritual development seeking to establish independence in things both spiritual and temporal? In our experience, almost always it was a mixture of a developing spiritual capacity to hear the voice of the Lord and an inclination to establish independence.

I emphasize an important point here. The adolescent-aged desire to establish spiritual and temporal independence is an essential part of our Heavenly

Father's divine design whereby we become "agents unto [ourselves],"[1] to act and not be "acted upon."[2] Because of that reality, while rearing our children Debbie and I never joked about "those horrible teenage years" or wished that we could "take away that darn agency" when our adolescent children made poor choices. Indeed, we saw the challenges that arose as unique, personal, spiritual insights being shared with us by Heavenly Father to assist us in rearing in truth and righteousness His spirit sons and daughters. Again, adolescents learning to hear and respond to the voice of the Spirit as they develop their capacity to righteously exercise agency is an essential, timely part of Heavenly Father's divine design for His children to become like Him.

As we continued with some loving questioning and meaningful discussion, the child eventually began to understand that "I just wanted to" could be better understood within the context of the choice so beautifully outlined in scripture: choosing to follow after one's own desires, or choosing to do the will of the Lord.

With additional brief discussion, a companion element usually became apparent: the disposition to fear man more than God. This was often expressed with words like the following: "I was having fun with my friends and they all wanted to stay out late, and I didn't want to be the one to end the fun."

As the Lord would make the heart of our child more fully known to us, our parental vision sharpened, and we could see the needs more clearly. Although we often were not entirely sure how to respond to those needs, two things we knew for sure were that the Lord would provide the answers and that the child needed to be closer to us for a period of time in order for the Spirit of the Lord to more fully influence them.

Our brief late-night discussion usually ended, therefore, with comments along the following lines:

"Mother and I know that the precious gift of the Holy Ghost is real. God promises that according to our faithfulness, the Holy Ghost will be our constant companion. We know that because we have experienced it. We also know that in the journey through life, there is only one sure way to find peace, safety, and joy, and that is through not only hearing, but having the courage and the will to hearken to the voice of the Lord, to obey the voice of the Spirit. Because of your choices tonight, we see that you would

1. Doctrine and Covenants 29:39.
2. 2 Nephi 2:14–15.

be blessed in gaining greater confidence in being able to do that better. Therefore, for a brief season, perhaps a few weeks, rather than you being out with your friends, we're going to have you here with us. During that time, we're going to do all we can to help you gain that greater confidence. You cannot imagine how much we want you to be with your friends, but to be with your friends once you and we know that you have not only the capacity to hear, but also the will and courage to respond to the voice of the Lord. That is the only sure way to safety and peace throughout your life."

Again, despite the several pages it has taken to describe this process, the late-night conversation only lasted about fifteen minutes. We wanted the children to feel our love, hear our testimonies of the workings of the Spirit, and go to bed knowing that there were spiritual things we were going to work on together.

It is important to note that such discussions with our children were kept confidential. We helped our children know we would keep their experiences and circumstances to ourselves, not sharing them with others in the family, unless there was an indicated need to share something and we all agreed to it, including the child involved. This built confidence and fostered trust between us and our children. It also provided a forum within which our children's individual spiritual learning could more easily occur.

This allowed our children to take ownership of their spiritual maturing, without feeling the need to publicly oppose the counsel being received from parents merely to protect their growing need for independence. Even more significantly, as parents we witnessed such experiences become important tools in our children's hands as they forged their own spiritual identities.

During the time the child was with us rather than friends, we did all we could to help the discipline to engender love and discipleship. Scripture study and prayer were always a part of the process. Fasting was sometimes a part. As parents, we sought the Lord's guidance to know what would best assist the child and reinforce in their hearts the recognition of divine spiritual communications and their confidence to follow them. Everything didn't always work out exactly the way we hoped, but we attempted to be unified and consistent in our efforts.

Sometimes we would suggest doctrine, principles, and scriptures we would review together. Sometimes we would ask our children to suggest what we could review together. This was separate and apart from our other continuing family religious practices.

CRAIG A. CARDON

Insofar as possible, adolescents and all of us are blessed when we understand the "why" of the Lord's commandments as we seek spiritual confirmation and affirmation of their truthfulness and validity. The "why" is found in doctrine and in understanding the plan of salvation, centered on the Atonement of the Lord Jesus Christ, with occasional help in suggesting practical, present-day application. The scriptures are a marvelous tool in such efforts, enhancing the opportunity for the Holy Ghost to fulfill His essential role in touching hearts and enlightening minds. The spiritual rewards we experienced with our children as we engaged in this effort often exceeded anything we might have initially anticipated as the discussions regularly involved other scriptural passages, sometimes unrelated to the first, that the children had been directed to by the Spirit.

An example of what we might do to initiate such discussions during the time our child was with us, rather than with friends, would be to ask our child to read the following scriptural references and then share with us what they had learned and felt as they studied and pondered them.

- Mosiah 6:1–2. (All but little children entered into a covenant with God.)
- Mosiah 26:1–4. (Many of the rising generation could not understand, did not believe, their hearts were hardened, they were a separate people, they would not call upon God.)
- 3 Nephi 1:28–30. (Much sorrow among the Lamanites, many children did grow up and became for themselves, led away by flattering words.)

The unique individual learning our children experienced during these focused reading and discussing opportunities regularly far exceeded the outward meaning of the words on the page.

As another example, we might ask that our child read the following scriptures and then share with us the spiritual connections they could make between these verses.

- Doctrine and Covenants 1:14–16. (There will be a day when people will not hear the voice of the Lord or of His prophets because they have strayed from ordinances and broken covenants, and men walk in their own way.)
- 3 Nephi 27:13; John 6:38. (The Savior came into the world to do the will of His Father.)

At appropriate points in their spiritual development, we sometimes invited our children to prepare from the scriptures a fifteen- to twenty-minute lesson to teach us about the Atonement of Jesus Christ. If they needed some assistance, it was given through asking them questions for which they could search out answers rather than providing answers directly.

In other instances we might provide some historical background for some scriptural passages, such as Doctrine and Covenants 3 (the Lord's rebuke of Joseph Smith and instruction to him after the loss of the 116 translated pages from the Book of Mormon), and then invite our children to read the scriptural passage and tell us what parallels they found in their own life experiences.

Our primary purpose in any of these exercises and in spending this special time with our children was to help them "feel" things as they made spirit-borne connections between their lives and the truths recorded in the scriptures. The scriptural knowledge being gained was helpful, but secondary. At this critical developmental time in their lives, we earnestly desired that the development of their spiritual capacities to feel and act be full and complete, rather than being quenched.

At the end of two or three weeks, or whatever time had been indicated with our child, it was like a little graduation experience to feel a peaceful confirmation rest with us and with our child that he or she was now better prepared and more willing to recognize and follow the promptings of the Spirit. We had no doubt that there would be future lessons yet to be learned. This is true for all of us as we progress throughout our lives. But it was a joy to see our children grow through these experiences in their capacity to recognize the voice of the Spirit and their willingness to hearken to that voice.

These experiences over the years fostered within our children a greater sense of their individual and personal responsibility for their spiritual development, for their capacity to recognize and respond to the voice of the Spirit. They also helped our children recognize the importance of holding sacred Heavenly Father's personal communications. Over the years, each child came to more fully understand their individual responsibility for their own conversion. This fostered within each of their hearts a greater love for the Lord and a deeper conversion to the Lord Jesus Christ and His gospel. All of this was more precious to them because of their essential, personal role in obtaining it.

Another important aspect of this process was our children's recognition that there was a higher purpose in discipline, which purpose was to help them to know the means and have the capacity to receive heavenly direction and find joy in this life.

Once again, we recognize that not all children respond quickly, and not all respond positively. Some may even knowingly and willfully rebel as they quench the Spirit with hardened hearts.

During the early part of the twentieth century, a young, non-Christian man from India by the name of Sadhu Sundar Singh experienced a dramatic and miraculous conversion to Christianity and thereafter devoted the remainder of his life to the sharing of the gospel as he understood it. After visiting America in 1920, he observed the following:

> Once when I was in the Himalayas, I was sitting upon the bank of a river; I drew out of the water a beautiful, hard, round stone and smashed it. The inside was quite dry. The stone had been lying a long time in the water, but the water had not penetrated the stone. It is just like that with the "Christian" people of the West. They have for centuries been surrounded by Christianity, entirely steeped in its blessings, but the Master's truth has not penetrated them.
>
> Christianity is not at fault; the reason lies rather in the hardness of their hearts. Materialism and intellectualism have made their hearts hard. So I am not surprised that many people in the West do not understand what Christianity really is.[3]

But hearts can be softened and penetrated. Parents, disheartened by seeing a child stray from the truth, sometimes speak of having done all they could do with their children, such as reading daily from the scriptures as a family, praying together, attending church together, and holding weekly family home evenings. Nonetheless, the child strayed. Frustrated after years of unheeded pleadings to their wayward child, parents may agonize over the agency their child is exercising and begin to "choose their battles," in the hope of communicating love, maintaining peace, and fostering association.

---

3. "Sadhu Sundar Singh: A Modern Day Apostle's Warning To America," by PRENTICE on APRIL 10, 2011. See more at: perkersonpark.com/2011/04/sadhu-sundar-singh-warns-america-stop-examining-spiritual-truths-like-dry-bones.html#sthash.ap0HYvaj.dpuf.

But we must be cautious and not simply allow children to stray and do what they want because they think they may have an eternity to come back. The objective for all of us, including our children, is to conform our will to the will of the Father—to change our desires to conform to the plan and purposes of the Lord. When they choose otherwise and stray from the covenant path, our duty is to lovingly, and with faith in Jesus Christ, do all possible to help them return. Occasionally, some parents seem to feel the need to move from choosing battles to a full retreat from the battlefield. Acknowledging that every circumstance is unique, and knowing that the Lord will inspire and direct, never give up hope. Although the Lord may prompt various and even changing methods of engagement, there is great value in continuing to trust in the Lord and not abandoning the battlefield.

Jesus taught, "It is easier for a camel to go through the eye of a needle, than for a rich man to enter into the kingdom of God." This caused His disciples to ask, "Who then can be saved?" Before recording the Savior's response, the scripture notes, "But Jesus beheld them." What a beautiful phrase! He saw them as they really were. He saw their uncertainty and their myopia, "and said unto them, With men this is impossible; but with God all things are possible."[4] Is God any less able to soften the heart of a wayward child than He is to soften the heart of a rich man and save him? The answer to the softening of a hard heart is not found in man's wisdom and reasoning. It is found in revelation from God.

As parents prayerfully seek guidance and insights to the state of their child's heart, the Lord will respond, often by providing "early warning" indicators evidenced through the child's exercise of agency. And as those indicators are revealed, every battle is worth fighting, albeit according to the Lord's time and the Lord's way, which He will also make known.

Through it all, we are brought to realize that there are no limits to the love and efforts of parents, other family members, and brothers and sisters in the gospel desiring to assist. Fasting and prayers in behalf of wayward souls never cease as parents and loved ones recognize that the conditions of this earthly existence are not neutral. There is opposition. And in faith, the battlefield is not abandoned.

In fostering the ability to recognize and respond to the voice of the Spirit, the Lord provides countless teaching moments and opportunities

---

4. Matthew 19:23–26.

for meaningful interventions, perhaps lasting no longer than the time to it takes to say a word, or to share a look, or to offer deserved praise. The point is that this focus of supporting our children's spiritual development must be constantly on our minds, in our hearts, and a part of our prayers. In my wife's and my experience, the Lord is abundantly gracious in helping us to recognize the teaching moments, and helping us know how to engage them, often communicating those things in the very moments they unfolded before us.

7

SEEKING INDEPENDENCE

EACH OF US HAS A PHYSICAL BODY and each of us has a spiritual body. The Lord explained to Joseph Smith, "The spirit and the body are the soul of man."[1] Abraham explains, "And the Gods formed man from the dust of the ground, and took his spirit (that is, the man's spirit), and put it into him; and breathed into his nostrils the breath of life, and man became a living soul."[2] And in the Old Testament, Elihu spoke to his three friends and to Job, saying, "There is a spirit in man: and the inspiration of the Almighty giveth them understanding."[3]

Each of us is not only a physical son or physical daughter of earthly parents. Each of us is also a spiritual son or a spiritual daughter of Heavenly Parents.[4] And we only have life in this earthly existence as our spirit bodies and our physical bodies remain united.

Our spirit bodies are the means through which we receive divine communications through the Light of Christ, through the power of the Holy Ghost, and through the gift of the Holy Ghost. The vital lesson of life is to learn to recognize these divine communications and to have the courage to respond to them.

Through the prophet Joseph Smith the Lord explained, "The Spirit giveth light to every man that cometh into the world; and the Spirit

---

1. Doctrine and Covenants 88:15.
2. Abraham 5:7.
3. Job 32:8.
4. "Each [of us] is a beloved spirit son or daughter of heavenly parents" ("The Family: A Proclamation to the World."

enlighteneth every man through the world, that hearkeneth to the voice of the Spirit."[5] He gave essentially the same message through John,[6] Paul,[7] Mormon,[8] and Moroni.[9]

Among the solemn and non-transferable duties God has given to parents is the essential element of teaching them to understand "the gift of the Holy Ghost by the laying on of the hands . . . . and . . . to pray, and to walk uprightly before the Lord."[10] Enoch gave a commandment that parents teach their children, saying, "Even so ye must be born again into the kingdom of heaven, of water, and of the Spirit."[11] Other loving and trusted adults assist parents in these divine responsibilities.

With this brief doctrinal background and review, it is helpful to note a few elements of the spiritual nature and development of children that are common to our shared experiences.

Primary children, ages three to eleven, easily and eagerly embrace spiritual things. They believe what their parents and other loving and trusted adults teach them. Because of their innocence, they are easily entreated by the Spirit. They "feel" spiritual things and willingly acknowledge it. They don't question. They accept.

As children move into adolescence, the teenage years, by divine design they begin to question. This means that along with many other physical and emotional changes, their disposition toward spiritual things changes. Rather than simply feeling and accepting, they question. There may be varying degrees of intensity, or scope, or breadth and depth of questioning. But as a divinely appointed part of their earthly experience, they question. They want to know for themselves rather than merely accepting what others know. This is a part of the continuing process by which they mature in their exercise of agency.

Many parents and other adult leaders have lamented these times, regularly wondering what has become of their previously "easily entreated" child. But I repeat, this developmental change during adolescence is by divine design. Notwithstanding the many challenges that it necessitates,

---

5. Doctrine and Covenants 84:46. See also Doctrine and Covenants 46:16.
6. John 1:9.
7. 1 Corinthians 12:7.
8. Moroni 7:16.
9. Moroni 10:17.
10. Doctrine and Covenants 68:25–26.
11. Moses 6:59.

this is a time of not only physical and emotional maturing, but even more importantly, it is a time of spiritual maturing. It is not a time to be lamented. It is an important, essential time that is to be knowingly and faithfully embraced.

Luke provides a one-verse description of the Savior's adolescent years: "And Jesus increased in wisdom and stature, and in favour with God and man."[12] *The Personal Development: Youth Guidebook* produced by The Church of Jesus Christ of Latter-day Saints references this enlightening verse and invites youth to follow the Savior's example in developing their lives in these four areas: spiritual (favour with God); social (favour with man); physical (stature); and intellectual (wisdom). This pattern of development recognizes the reality of adolescents' divinely appointed search for independence, which allows them eventually to stand accountable before God. As the Lord emphasizes, "For the power is in them, wherein they are agents unto themselves."[13] While recognizing the importance and significance of these four areas, for the purposes of this book, I am focusing here more specifically on spiritual and physical independence, as well as emotional independence, which is an important element embedded in all four areas.

Simply stated, adolescents seek independence. It is during these years that they establish their independence through their developing capacity to exercise agency. All of this becomes an important part of their personal identity that will define much of the remainder of their lives. And while much has and should be said in many quarters about the importance of helping youth in their divinely appointed quest to form their physical and emotional identity, all too often, parents and other adults may not fully comprehend their responsibilities in helping youth form their spiritual identity, leaving it more to happenstance than to objective purpose.

Part of the issue for parents is the constancy and difficulty of the task, due in large part to the tension or even conflict that sometimes occurs between parents and adolescents on matters relating to independence. A couple of graphs may aid understanding.

---

12. Luke 2:52.
13. Doctrine and Covenants 58:28.

SEEKING INDEPENDENCE GRAPH 1

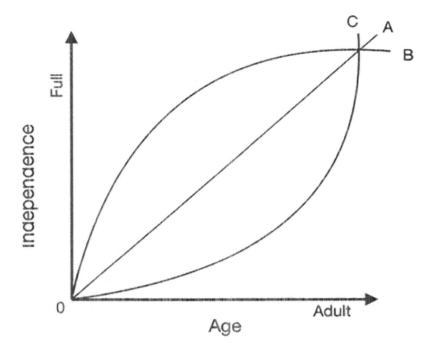

In Graph 1, line A represents what some may consider to be an ideal developmental path of independence, whether spiritual, physical, or emotional, and I will add here, financial, as it may help conceptualize the principle. At birth, a newborn child is completely dependent on others for everything. Then, on an evenly measured trajectory, the child develops greater independence with age, ideally becoming completely independent at the age of adulthood. Line B represents the trajectory adolescents often think they are capable of experiencing, should be on, and should be recognized by their parents or guardians. Line C represents the trajectory parents or guardians often think adolescents are capable of following, are actually on, and should be recognized by the adolescents.

SEEKING INDEPENDENCE GRAPH 2

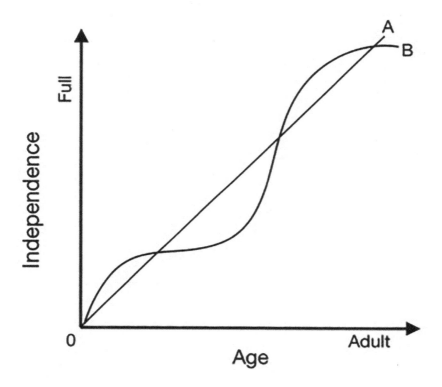

In Graph 2, line A again represents what some may consider to be an ideal developmental path of independence. Line B represents what may the actual developmental path of an adolescent. If separate lines were used to represent spiritual, physical, emotional, and financial independence for an individual, it is highly likely that each line would follow a different trajectory (see Graph 3). And when considering multiple individuals maturing in a single family, the actual varying trajectories would significantly complicate the graph (see Graph 4). But indeed, this is the reality engaged by parents and guardians rearing children.

SEEKING INDEPENDENCE GRAPH 3

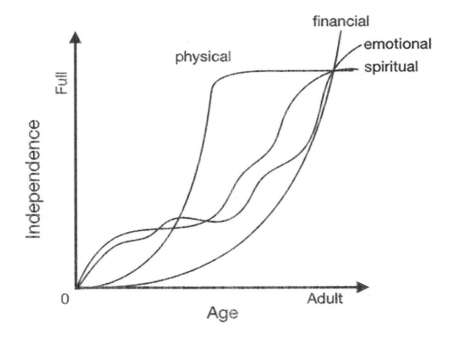

Graph 3 represents what the different developmental trajectories may look like for the spiritual, physical, emotional, and financial development of an adolescent.

SEEKING INDEPENDENCE GRAPH 4

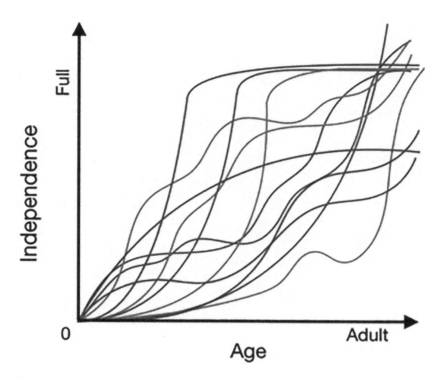

Graph 4 represents the potential complexity of development patterns for multiple adolescents in a single family, with lines representing multiple developmental trajectories for various family members.

Notwithstanding the constancy, difficulty, and the uniqueness of each child's path, lovingly and effectively helping an adolescent navigate the waters of developing independence, especially spiritual independence, is one of a parent's most important responsibilities.

Dr. Lisa Miller is a professor of psychology and education and is the director of the Clinical Psychology Program at Columbia University, Teachers College. She is not a member of The Church of Jesus Christ of Latter-day Saints. I had the opportunity to meet and visit with her a few years ago when she visited Salt Lake City shortly after the publishing of her book, *The Spiritual Child: The New Science on Parenting for Health and Lifelong Thriving.* In her book she states:

> On the strength of empirical research, we now know that spirituality is indeed part of our natural endowment, just like our abilities to see, smell, and think. Spirituality is experienced through a biologically based faculty and we are born ready to use it; we enter the world prepared to have a spiritual life. Science also shows that while we are born inherently spiritual, this faculty can be sustained and cultivated by parents or dulled by neglect.[14]

The divine design in developing spiritual maturity is known also to the adversary. Knowing of how critically important this development is in all that will follow as the adolescent continues through life, because of the adversary's influence, the world begins to communicate a relentless message to adolescents: "The spiritual voice you heard and felt as a child is not real. It is only your imagination. It cannot be trusted. Don't listen to it. It is not real."

Because of this, while patterns of regular individual and family prayer, scripture study, and worship are so important, without conscious and inspired efforts by parents to help their children recognize the spiritual communications received while participating in those activities and to act on them, a central role of the activity is being missed. Ultimately, the goal is much more than having our children knowledgeable of the scriptural account, the ordinances, and how to pray. The goal is for them to hear, recognize, and respond to the voice of the Spirit, relying on that voice and joyously accepting the fact that religious activities foster divine communications.

---

14. Lisa Miller, *The Spiritual Child: The New Science on Parenting for Health and Lifelong Thriving* (New York: St. Martin's Press, 2015), 51–52.

These activities are also important for parents seeking to fulfill their divinely appointed roles as fathers and mothers. Significantly, while these activities are being experienced by family members, through the exercise of faith in the Lord and fervent prayer, the Lord reveals to parents early warning signs indicating the dispositions of their children's hearts to spiritual things. He also inspires parents in how to engage the unique circumstances as a child may begin to show signs of quenching the Spirit.

An experience we had with Craig, our third child and our eldest son, illustrates many of these principles. First, some background.

Since beginning our family, Debbie and I had worked diligently to make our home a place of gospel learning and spiritual development amidst the normal rough and tumble of daily family life. This included the essential elements of personal and family scripture study and personal and family prayer. Debbie and I would arise early and have our individual prayers. We would gather the family members, usually beginning at 6:00 a.m., for family scripture reading from the Book of Mormon and family prayer. We weren't perfect in this, but we were generally consistent on Mondays through Fridays, sporadic on Saturdays, and found another time on Sundays depending on changing meeting schedules. Every family member had an individual copy of the Book of Mormon, and we would take turns reading verses, depending on age and reading ability.

When an infant child could not read, Debbie, one of the older children, or I would hold the infant and would, with one of the infant's index fingers, point to each word as it was read. If it was the infant's turn to read, the one helping him or her would say each word for the infant and allow the infant to mimic the word. Sometimes this was just for one phrase or sentence, while others may have read up to several verses.

After reading, we would all kneel together in a circle and have family prayer, again with each family member in turn having opportunity to be voice in the prayer. After the family prayer, we enjoyed the practice of having the youngest child go to the center of the circle while the rest of us put our arms around each other, or attempted to do so as the restless boys began poking and wrestling with each other and teasing their sisters. Finally, we would all lean toward the center, and while slightly squeezing the person on each side, say in unison, "Faaaaaaaamily hug!" Then, hopefully, with most of us remaining upright after the good-natured group hug, we would drop our arms to our sides, lean in even further, and testing the limits of what brothers and sisters could tolerate, put our heads cheek-to-cheek and say, "Faaaaaaaamily kiss!" with a big open-air smooch to the center, with most everyone trying to give the youngest child in the middle an actual kiss. This usually led to more children falling over, while the youngest child always loved and anticipated this special moment of combined family attention.

The children would then go to their rooms for their morning individual prayers, if they had not already offered them. As was common in those days, the girls were always rushing to find the time to eat breakfast and do their hair before running out the door for school. Debbie and I would help the younger children with their prayers. And we would encourage the children to find time during the day to spend a few minutes in the scriptures individually. For the older children, this was often accomplished during Seminary. Today, "Come, Follow Me" beautifully fosters this study.

In the evening, we would kneel around the dinner table or in the family room for family prayer, followed by the same family hug and family kiss. We taught our children to express gratitude and to ask for the Lord's blessing on the food they ate. We would regularly confirm that the children were saying their evening individual prayers before retiring to bed. Debbie and I would do the same, sometimes praying together to seek guidance, strength, and blessings for our family.

The purpose in all of this was to help our children connect with heaven. Learning doctrine, knowing the scriptural stories, being familiar with kneeling prayer and the language of prayer were important and were given much attention, but they were secondary. Our primary objective was to help our children connect with heaven, to recognize the spiritual communications that would come to them, and to have the courage to respond to those communications as the Lord directed.

Craig was fifteen years old at the time of the following experience. Seven of our eight children were living at home. The oldest was away at college. The youngest was three years old. I had been serving as a stake president for over three years. At this time there were significant economic challenges confronting the entire nation, and our entrepreneurial interests were not immune. Notwithstanding my demanding schedule, Debbie was able to be at home with the children. As had been the case throughout our marriage, her spiritual sensitivity to otherwise slight fluctuations in the flow of our children's lives was a significant and important factor in our parental role of rearing our children.

As I recall, I had missed the evening meal with the family, which happened from time to time, when I rushed into our home from work one evening, with just enough time to grab a bite to eat before heading off to Church meetings. When I greeted Debbie with a kiss, with an unexpected degree of intensity she told me that she needed to talk to me. It was a communication that I had long since learned to pay attention to. Nonetheless, I asked if it could wait. She was willing to wait but expressed her feeling that it would be best not to wait. I had also long since learned to respect her impressions on timing. We stepped into another room for privacy.

Debbie said that over the past several days she had noticed that whenever Craig and I talked with each other, there was a degree of tension in the conversation that had not previously been present. I told her that I hadn't noticed anything particularly different. She said that while that may be, she had noticed that Craig was beginning to react a bit differently. She couldn't give any specific examples. It was just more of a feeling that she had sensed in him and that had come to her.

I suggested that perhaps this was what occurs normally when two males visit with each other. This thought did not subdue the feelings Debbie was having. There was something more occurring in my communications with Craig that was not easily identified. With Debbie, I began to feel that there was something here that needed to be addressed. But we didn't know what it was or how to address it. We decided to pray.

Over the ensuing days, as we prayed about this matter and counseled together, the Lord brought a detail to my attention of which I had not been previously cognizant. In almost every conversation Craig and I were having, we were expressing opposing opinions on topics for which one or the other of us had a vested interest. And because of the vested interest and differing opinion, there was a degree of tension.

The Lord had now revealed to us the problem. But what were we to do? How could this problem be addressed to the blessing of all involved? We continued to pray.

Eventually, an impression came to my mind that I shared with Debbie. The impression was to schedule a private time each day with Craig, twenty to thirty minutes, where he and I would talk together under certain rules. With the impression the Lord also provided rules for the meeting. The rules were as follow:

- We would meet in the small room near our front door that I used for a home office, and we would alternate offering an opening prayer for each meeting.
- One of us would be responsible to identify a new topic at the beginning of each meeting that we would explore together.
- The responsibility for choosing a topic would alternate between us each meeting.
- In every discussion, one of us would be obligated to speak in favor of the topic, the other in opposition.
- Significantly, the person identifying the topic was also authorized to specify who would speak in favor and who would speak in opposition, and who would speak first.
- While the topic could be of interest to one or both of us, it had to be a topic in which neither of us had any vested interest at all.
- If the person responsible for choosing the topic came to the meeting without a topic in mind, he was obligated to choose a current topic from the first section of the morning newspaper.

That was it. Simple. Straight forward.

As for the timing of the meeting, Craig was, and still is, an early riser. While this may not be true for many adolescents, it was not a stretch to suggest to Craig that we meet at 5:30 a.m. With prayerful consideration, I proposed to Craig that we meet with the rules as described above. He initially wondered why such an exercise was necessary, but when I mentioned what Mother had been observing and feeling, he also more fully recognized the tension that had been developing and agreed to meet.

I will acknowledge that I was amazed at the rapid progress we made. Within just days, some remarkable things happened. We were both learning that the other of us was able to see at least two sides of just about any topic. We were both learning that we could hear opposing views from the other person and respect those views, although we may not agree with them. Admittedly, this was occurring with topics in which neither of us had a vested interest, but there was developing between us a respectful maturity of friendly persuasion. And it was responding in a positive, reinforcing way to Craig's desire for emotional independence.

But there was an even greater spiritual blessing that neither Craig nor I could have anticipated.

With the great progress that had been made after just a few days, Craig walked into our meeting with a slight smile on his face. After prayer, we both sat down, face-to-face and nearly knee-to-knee. It was his turn to identify the topic. But he wanted to discuss something before doing so. The dialogue went something like this:

"Dad, before we get started I'd like to change one of the rules."

"Okay, Son. I think that's something we can at least discuss. What rule would you like to change and how would you like to change it?"

With his smile growing a bit bigger, he replied, "No, Dad. I want you to agree to the change first, and then I'll tell you what the change is."

We had made such marvelous progress. Trust, confidence, and respect between us had grown. In a certain way, Craig was testing all of these things. As I looked at him, although quite uncertain as to where this might lead, with a bit of a smile of my own and with a degree of uncertainty I responded.

"Well, Craig, this is going to be a stretch, but let's give it a try. The change is approved. What is it?"

His smile was now complete.

"The change is that today we will address a topic that one of us has a vested interest in. All other rules remain the same. This is the topic: 'Is it okay for a fifteen-year-old to date?' Dad, you speak in favor and I'll speak against, and Dad, you go first!"

I was slightly stunned. What had I gotten myself into? It will be no surprise to know that this and related topics had fostered much of the tension in Craig's and my earlier communications that Debbie had originally identified. But here we were, and I had agreed to the change.

My mind began to race with the realization that I would be speaking as both a father and a stake president. I don't remember exactly what I said. Neither does Craig. Generally, I believe I attempted to describe unique circumstances that would be difficult to duplicate and added many qualifiers and disclaimers. I imagine that I concluded by allowing that under those unique circumstances and conditions, possibly, it could be acceptable for a fifteen-year-old to date.

Craig had watched me as I was speaking with his elbows on his knees and his hands clasped in front of him, and although he was looking at me, I wasn't sure what he was hearing. I spoke for several minutes. As I did, his expression began to change. When I concluded, he looked at me just a moment longer, and then his eyes went to the floor. He was silent. I could not read his expression because I could see only the top of his head. I waited for a few moments in silence. After about twenty to thirty seconds, I spoke. "Son, I've finished what I was going to say. Now it's your turn. Why is it not okay for a fifteen-year-old to date?"

With his elbows still on his knees and his hands still clasped, he lifted his head. Tears were now streaming down his cheeks and falling to the floor. In this instance, the tears were consistent with the Spirit of the Lord that was present in rich abundance. Eventually, Craig looked me straight in the eyes and with a resolute voice said simply, "Because a prophet said not to!"

Something miraculous had just happened that neither one of us had anticipated. Craig, questioning, seeking independence, wanting to know for himself, had just received an independent witness from his Heavenly Father on a personal matter of immense importance to him that provided a course correction in his heart and life. At this critical juncture, he had heard the voice of the Lord and had responded in faith.

And in the process, the Lord had blessed a father and a son with new-found capacities to communicate with respect and understanding on all topics, with or without one or the other having a vested interest.

Craig's spiritual resolve and independence were significantly strengthened that day. This was more important than the emotional resolve and independence that accompanied the experience. He now had a much greater capacity to recognize and to respond to the voice of the Spirit.

I also learned how intimately involved the Lord is in helping parents and trusted adult leaders in their efforts to help the rising generation connect with Him. It is His work, and as a loving Father, He is anxious to communicate with His children.

8

THE WORLD'S PRESSURE
TO CONFORM

ONE OF THE ADVERSARY'S MOST EFFECTIVE TOOLS in getting sons and daughters of God to "quench the Spirit," especially those of adolescent and young adult age, is to exert peer pressure, the pressure of a group to conform to the norms of the group that are inconsistent with the Lord's purposes. In today's world, this pressure is often applied directly through social media and indirectly through both social and mass media. However, its most immediate and compromising effect regularly occurs through face-to-face associations within groups.

Because this pressure to conform is so pervasive and prevalent in all of our lives, it is important for all to understand how powerful the influence can be, often without anything being said directly to the one being influenced. However, it is also encouraging to learn how, in critical moments, a single person in a group willing to do the right thing can be a powerful influence for good, and to know that there are many opportunities to be the one providing that influence. These two perspectives are highlighted in some conformity experiments conducted decades ago by Solomon Asch.

Solomon Eliot Asch was a pioneer in social psychology in the United States.[1] In 1951 he conducted his first conformity laboratory experiments at Swarthmore College near Philadelphia. The following Wikipedia report

---

1. "Solomon Asch," Wikipedia, en.wikipedia.org/wiki/Solomon_Asch, accessed May 13, 2020.

provides a summary of Asch's first experiment, which provided evidence of this pressure to conform.[2]

Groups of eight male college students participated in a simple "perceptual" task. In reality, all but one of the participants were actors, and the true focus of the study was about how the remaining participant would react to the actors' behavior.

The actors knew the true aim of the experiment, but were introduced to the subject as other participants. Each student viewed a card with a line on it, followed by another with three lines labeled *A*, *B*, and *C* (see accompanying figure). One of these lines was the same as that on the first card, and the other two lines were clearly longer or shorter (i.e. a near-100% rate of correct responding was expected). Each participant was then asked to say aloud which line matched the length of that on the first card. Before the experiment, all actors were given detailed instructions on how they should respond to each trial (card presentation). They would always unanimously nominate one comparator, but on certain trials they would give the correct response and on others, an incorrect response. The group was seated such that the real participant always responded last.

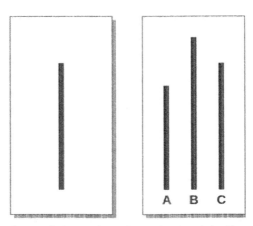

One of the pairs of cards used in the experiment. The card on the left has the reference line and the one on the right shows the three comparison lines.

---

2. "Asch conformity experiments," Wikipedia, accessed May 13, 2020. en.wikipedia.org/wiki/Asch_conformity_experiments; emphasis added.

[The] subjects completed 18 trials. On the first two trials, both the subject and the actors gave the obvious, correct answer. On the third trial, the actors would all give the same wrong answer. This wrong-responding recurred on 11 of the remaining 15 trials. It was the subjects' behavior on these 12 "critical trials" that formed the aim of the study: to test how many subjects would change their answer to conform to those of the 7 actors, despite it being wrong. Subjects were interviewed after the study including being debriefed about the true purpose of the study. These post-test interviews shed valuable light on the study . . . because they revealed subjects often were "just going along. . . . "

Asch's experiment also had a condition in which participants were tested alone with only the experimenter in the room. In total, there were 50 subjects in the experimental condition and 37 in the control condition.

In the control group, with no pressure to conform to actors, the error rate of the critical stimuli was less than 1%.

In the actor condition also, the majority of participants' responses remained correct (63.2%), but a sizeable minority of responses conformed to the actors' (incorrect) answer (36.8%). The responses revealed strong individual differences: Only 5 percent of participants were always swayed by the crowd. 25 percent . . . consistently defied majority opinion, with the rest conforming on some trials. An examination of all critical trials in the experimental group revealed that one-third of all responses were incorrect. These incorrect responses often matched the incorrect response of the majority group (i.e., actors). **Overall, 75% of participants gave at least one incorrect answer out of the 12 critical trials.**

Imagine the strength of the influence of a group upon the members of the group to conform! On a visual perceptual test, using comparisons that were patently obvious and would normally elicit 100 percent correct responses, 75 percent of the respondents gave at least one wrong answer, principally due to the pressure to conform to the group perception. That is a startling statistic.

However, in a subsequent test, Asch added an element that would provide powerful evidence of the positive influence for good a single individual can have in a group. Once again, Wikipedia summarizes:

In subsequent research experiments, Asch explored several variations on the paradigm from his 1951 study.

In 1955 he reported on work with 123 male students from three different universities. A second paper in 1956 also consisted of 123 male college students from three different universities. Asch did not state if this was in fact the same sample as reported in his 1955 paper: The principal difference is that the 1956 paper includes an elaborate account of his interviews with participants. Across all these papers, Asch found the same results: participants conformed to the majority group in about one-third of all critical trials.

[However, in an added variation,] Asch found that the presence of a "true partner" (a "real" participant or another actor told to give the correct response to each question) decreased conformity. *In studies that had one actor give correct responses to the questions, only 5% of the participants continued to answer with the majority.[3]*

Consider the significance and power of the influence of the "presence of a true partner" in a group upon the real participant in the group. When another person in the group gave the right answer, the percentage of real participants on at least one occasion giving an obviously wrong answer dropped from 75 percent to 5 percent. Knowing there was someone else in the group who could recognize the correct answer and was willing to express it in front of others giving wrong answers gave enough courage to the real participant who also recognized the right answer to express it publicly.

While there may be many lessons to be drawn from this reality, two significant lessons for all of us are: 1) the importance and value of us being a true partner for others, and 2) the importance and value of choosing and associating with good friends who will be true partners for us, recognizing and acting on what is right at critical moments in furthering the Lord's purposes.

The Savior expressed being a "true partner" this way to the people in Bountiful: "Therefore, hold up your light that it may shine unto the world. Behold, I am the light which ye shall hold up—that which ye have seen me do."[4]

At appropriate times in their lives, we as parents attempted to help our children understand these principles and develop the courage to follow them. We invited them to be a "true partner" in every group they were in and to speak up at appropriate times in giving right answers. We helped them see that in doing so, they would be fortifying others in the

---

3. Ibid.; emphasis added.
4. 3 Nephi 18:24.

group to speak up for what is right, others who might otherwise succumb to the pressure to conform to wrong answers.

When our oldest child, Tricia, was in the fifth grade, she came home from school one day with exciting news. In the following story, try to comprehend this fifth-grade method of communicating: One of Tricia's girlfriends, Rachel (all names except family names have been changed), informed her that Ben, a popular boy in their class, had asked his friend, Tony, to inform Rachel that Ben liked Tricia and planned in the near future to ask her to go steady with him!

Tricia's friends were excited for her, and all of Ben's friends were anxious to see what Tricia would say. Tricia didn't fully understand what "going steady" meant, and I suspect Ben didn't either, but whatever else it meant for these boys and girls, Tricia understood that in part it meant restricting her social contacts and associations with other boys in her class and school and creating an "exclusive" relationship with Ben. We quickly learned that several of Tricia's friends, some of them the children of our friends and associates, were already "going steady," with their parents having deemed the practice to be "cute" and an innocent expression of childhood infatuation. From some other parents we later heard justifications for allowing the practice that included "everybody's doing it" and "what could be the harm?" At an age much younger than we had anticipated as new parents, we found our first child, this precious daughter, facing a social practice that seemed innocent enough to many, but that we recognized to have significant implications for how Tricia would face social pressures in the future, especially during her adolescent years and beyond.

Not knowing exactly how to address this, Debbie and I went to the Lord. At its core, the impressions came to address the underlying principle. Founded in the counsel of the prophets that youth not begin dating until age sixteen, we sought to see what the prophets were seeing. We were not child psychologists, but we were parents and we had the promise of the Lord's help as we sought direction. We looked at our precious ten-year-old daughter and saw a valiant spirit, maturing in many ways, but as yet unable to adequately anticipate what it would mean to her social development to exclude contact and association with other males in deference to one boy at such a young age, or to accurately and capably process her and the boy's emotions and interactions that would be heightened and sensitized by exclusive contact. Perhaps more importantly, we also saw this as a meaningful opportunity to help Tricia establish a pattern in her young life of seeking spiritual confirmation in decisions of consequence in her life. As we began to see and feel these things, we desired that our Tricia would also be able to see and feel them.

As directed by the Spirit, we met with Tricia. At a level she could understand we talked about how important it was for boys and girls to learn how to interact with each other and to respect each other. We talked about what dating was and how the prophets had counseled that dating not begin before age sixteen. We explained that going steady was something that came even later than dating. We noted that while she had a marvelous capacity to understand and process many of her life's experiences, with age and more experience her capacity would grow, and this would be important as she engaged others in future years, especially those of the opposite sex.

As we talked, we asked Tricia questions to determine what she was understanding and to know what was occurring in her heart and mind. While she was gaining understanding about the importance of girls and boys learning to interact with many personalities in groups and the social skill development and emotional maturing that might be lost through "going steady" exclusion, it soon became clear that she was worrying about the embarrassment that might come to Ben and even to her if she simply said no. With these expressions, we realized that we had moved from the principles associated with the wisdom of the prophets to the age-old challenge of peer pressure to conform to the wishes of a group, even when the group is making poor choices. We've already noted that peer pressure to conform to the world is one of the adversary's favorite Spirit quenchers. For Tricia, we saw that doing what Mom and Dad said, or doing what the prophets said, would be founded in faith and would be good. However, adding to that the spiritual maturity to be able to independently recognize the voice of the Spirit and to have the courage to hearken to that voice, no matter the peer pressure, would be critical to her future testimony, safety, peace, and happiness.

As we talked about the principles associated with social interactions between girls and boys of her age and assessed her understanding, we also asked about what she was feeling. We spoke with her about times in our lives when we were her age and felt spiritual promptings and communications. She let us know that she was feeling those things, as well. She was receiving her own, independent spiritual confirmation that going steady was not the right thing to do. She was beginning to act, not "because Mom and Dad said," or even because "the prophets said." She was well informed on both of those counts, but she was now acting on the basis of what the Spirit was confirming to her. This was her decision, not the decision of another. She owned it, spiritually and every other way. We then talked about the courage it often takes to follow impressions of the Spirit. But how to do that was important. We came up with a plan.

From among our older nieces and nephews, Debbie and I had seen some rather creative ways of older adolescents inviting friends to formal dances and creative ways of accepting such invitations. While this had been beyond Tricia's experience, in our counseling with her, creative options were made available to her for how she might apply the principles, of which she now had her own testimony. An option that Tricia liked quickly surfaced: she could place a written response in a balloon that Ben would have to pop in order to read.

The next day, at recess Tony ran over to Tricia's group and said in front of everyone, "Trish, Ben wants to know if you will go steady with him." All the girls immediately looked at Tricia in anticipation. Tricia responded, "Tell Ben his answer will come in a mysterious way." Surprised, but delighted, Tony ran back to Ben's group and within everyone's hearing conveyed the message.

Tricia came home from school and asked her mother to help her draft the note. They went through a few drafts, eventually settling on words something like the following: "Ben, I think you are great. Thanks for asking me to go steady. I'm not going to date until I'm sixteen, and I won't go steady until after that. If I were going to go steady, it would be with a guy like you. I hope we can still be friends. Tricia"

As they were completing the note, Ben unexpectedly came to our home, escorting his two younger brothers who wanted to play with Tricia's younger brother. Tricia and her mom quickly put the note in a balloon and inflated it. Tricia took the balloon outside and gave it to Ben and told him to look inside. As she stood nervously by, with some excitement Ben popped the balloon and grabbed the note that fell to the ground. He read it silently and smiled. He then turned to Tricia and with the smile still on his face and his confidence and dignity intact, he said simply, "Okay." That was it. The response had been delivered, and Ben was happy.

When Tricia went back to school the next day, she saw that the word of the mysterious response had spread quickly, with universal acceptance.

Although the invitation to go steady had not been accepted, because of the genuine, complimentary language of the note, everyone was fine with it. Indeed, because of the gentleness and respect with which it was handled, the interest seemed to be more in the way it was communicated with the balloon. And, as a happy added benefit, Tricia and Ben remained friends. The Spirit of the Lord had blessed the lives of everyone involved.

In Lehi's dream of the tree of life, the spacious building was "filled with people, both old and young, both male and female . . . in the attitude of mocking and pointing their fingers towards those who had come at and were partaking of the fruit."[5]

It takes strength to be the one standing for truth. Jacob showed that strength when confronted by Sherem, a man who was seeking to "overthrow the doctrine of Christ":

> And [Sherem] was learned, that he had a perfect knowledge of the language of the people; wherefore, he could use much flattery, and much power of speech, according to the power of the devil.
>
> And he had hope to shake me from the faith, notwithstanding the many revelations and the many things which I had seen concerning these things; for I truly had seen angels, and they had ministered unto me. And also, I had heard the voice of the Lord speaking unto me in very word, from time to time; wherefore, I could not be shaken.[6]

Not all valiant people will see angels, but they can and must have "many revelations." They can and must see "many things" concerning the trials they are facing, and they can and must hear "the voice of the Lord speaking unto them." Consider the significance of Jacob's words later in this account: "But behold, the Lord God poured in his Spirit into my soul, insomuch that I did confound [Sherem] in all his words."[7]

It was God's Spirit on which Jacob relied and by which he was guided, strengthened, and protected. That same spirit guided Tricia in her fifth-grade trial and also guided us as parents. Guidance, strength, and protection are available to all of us if we will resist spirit-quenching temptations to conform with the world and instead follow the living prophets and the promptings we will receive.

---

5. 1 Nephi 8:27.
6. Jacob 7:1–5.
7. Jacob 7:8.

9

PRAYER AND SCRIPTURES

OUR HEAVENLY FATHER HAS COMMANDED US TO pray unto Him in the name of His Only Begotten Son, Jesus Christ, with the promise that whatsoever we ask that is right shall be given to us.[1] The Savior also taught that when we ask in faith, believing that we shall receive, it is the Holy Ghost that "manifesteth all things which are expedient unto the children of men."[2] In learning how to recognize and respond to the voice of the Spirit, it is essential that we learn to pray in faith with the confidence that the Lord will respond by the voice of His Spirit, according to His will, as He has promised. Prayer, therefore, is central to this spiritual communication. There is no substitute for prayer.

When the Savior appeared to the people on the American continent following His resurrection, He taught them to pray, by precept and by example.

> He commanded the multitude that they should kneel upon the ground . . . .
>
> And . . . they knelt upon the ground. . . . And . . . he himself also knelt upon the earth; and behold he prayed unto the Father. . . .
>
> And . . . eye hath never seen, neither hath the ear heard, before, so great and marvelous things as ... Jesus [spake] unto the Father. . . .
>
> And . . . when Jesus had made an end of praying unto the Father, he arose.[3]

---

1. 3 Nephi 18:18–20.
2. Doctrine and Covenants 18:18.
3. 3 Nephi 17:13–18.

The Savior later emphasized these things with His disciples and again with the multitude.

> Verily, verily, I say unto you, ye must watch and pray always, lest ye be tempted by the devil, and ye be led away captive by him.
>
> And as I have prayed among you even so shall ye pray in my church. . . .
>
> And it came to pass that when Jesus had spoken these words unto his disciples, he turned again unto the multitude and said unto them:
>
> Behold, verily, verily, I say unto you, ye must watch and pray always lest ye enter into temptation: for Satan desireth to have you, that he may sift you as wheat.
>
> Therefore ye must always pray unto the Father in my name.[4]

This teaching was not passive. Directly and purposefully, the Savior taught the people to pray, and emphasized it on several occasions. The Savior promised, "If thou shalt ask, thou shalt receive revelation upon revelation, knowledge upon knowledge, that thou mayest know the mysteries and the peaceable things—that which bringeth joy, that which bringeth life eternal. Thou shalt ask, and it shall be revealed unto you in mine own due time."[5]

The Savior also made known how the revelations, knowledge, mysteries, and peaceable things will come to us: "But the Comforter, which is the Holy Ghost, whom the Father will send in my name, he shall teach you all things, and bring all things to your remembrance, whatsoever I have said unto you."[6]

The Holy Ghost is the means through which Heavenly Father speaks to us. It is through this witness of the Spirit that we are converted to the gospel of Jesus Christ and sustained in the challenges of mortality. It is by means of the Spirit that God enlightens the faithful and makes known unto them the secrets of His will. In a preamble to the glorious vision of the degrees of glory, the Lord said to Joseph Smith and Sidney Rigdon:

> For thus saith the Lord—I, the Lord, am merciful and gracious unto those who fear me, and delight to honor those who serve me in righteousness and in truth unto the end.
>
> Great shall be their reward and eternal shall be their glory.

---

4. 3 Nephi 18:15–19.
5. Doctrine and Covenants 42:61–62.
6. John 14:26.

And to them will I reveal all mysteries, yea, all the hidden mysteries of my kingdom from days of old, and for ages to come, will I make known unto them the good pleasure of my will concerning all things pertaining to my kingdom.

Yea, even the wonders of eternity shall they know, and things to come will I show them, even the things of many generations.

And their wisdom shall be great, and their understanding reach to heaven; and before them the wisdom of the wise shall perish, and the understanding of the prudent shall come to naught.

For by my Spirit will I enlighten them, and by my power will I make known unto them the secrets of my will—yea, even those things which eye has not seen, nor ear heard, nor yet entered into the heart of man.[7]

As a companion to prayer, the Lord has provided the scriptures. During His mortal ministry the Lord made a revealing declaration to the unbelieving Jews that is relevant to us in our day: "Search the scriptures; for in them ye think ye have eternal life: and they are they which testify of me."[8]

What are we to understand from the phrase "for in them ye think ye have eternal life"? Having moved from the spirit to the letter of the law, the Jewish leaders were more focused on the outward task of parsing the scriptures than they were on opening their hearts to understanding the purpose for which the scriptures were given—to testify of the Son of God. It was for them as if the act of studying the scriptures, in and of itself, would bring them eternal life, without acknowledging the very purpose for which the scriptures exist and allowing the testimony of the Savior to sink into their souls. The Savior taught them plainly that the scriptures testify of Him. And how else are the scriptures able to testify of Jesus Christ, but through the ministry of the Holy Ghost? The Jewish leaders were reading the scriptures, but they were not hearing the voice of the Lord.

The Apostle Paul taught this important truth: "Wherefore I give you to understand, that no man speaking by the Spirit of God calleth Jesus accursed: and that no man can say that Jesus is the Lord, but by the Holy Ghost."[9]

---

7. Doctrine and Covenants 76:5–10.
8. John 5:39.
9. 1 Corinthians 12:3.

Notwithstanding their study of the scriptures, unwilling to feel the witness of the Holy Ghost, the Jewish leaders were unable to recognize the Son of God, even as they stood in His presence.

Near the end of his writing of the gospel, John records something that expresses the heart of every true prophet of God: "But these things are written, that ye might believe that Jesus is the Christ, the Son of God; and that believing ye might have life through his name."[10]

That is why the scriptures exist. And there is no substitute for the study of the scriptures with open hearts and minds, allowing us to hear the Spirit of the Lord testify of Jesus Christ, the Son of God.

Therefore, to not become like those who thought there was eternal life in the mere outward study of the scriptures, in our personal and family reading and pondering of the scriptures, it is essential that the connection be made with the Spirit of the Lord, for that is the means by which the scriptures bear witness.

The Book of Mormon: Another Testament of Jesus Christ is a particularly powerful tool given in these latter days to assist God's children in learning to recognize and to respond to the voice of the Spirit. Given as a sign that the Father has begun to fulfill His covenant to gather Israel,[11] the Book of Mormon is unique to this dispensation. By miraculous means the Lord provided this sacred record to help us become familiar with His voice and be converted to the gospel of Jesus Christ. So powerful is the witness of the Spirit to those who read, ponder, and pray about the Book of Mormon with real intent, that following the counsel and trusting in the promises made in the book tutors us in recognizing and responding to the Spirit as we become familiar with this divine means of communication. Indeed, none of us can be fully converted to the restored gospel of Jesus Christ and know and taste of His goodness through the ministry of the Spirit without receiving from the Holy Ghost the personal confirmation that the book and its message are true. Moroni communicated this as clearly as he could:

> Behold, I would exhort you that when ye shall read these things, if it be wisdom in God that ye should read them, that ye would remember how merciful the Lord hath been unto the children of men, from the creation of Adam even down until the time that ye shall receive these things, and ponder it in your hearts.

---

10. John 20:31.
11. 3 Nephi 21:1–7.

And when ye shall receive these things, I would exhort you that ye would ask God, the Eternal Father, in the name of Christ, if these things are not true; and if ye shall ask with a sincere heart, with real intent, having faith in Christ, he will manifest the truth of it unto you, by the power of the Holy Ghost.

And by the power of the Holy Ghost ye may know the truth of all things.

And whatsoever thing is good is just and true; wherefore nothing that is good denieth the Christ, but acknowledgeth that he is.

And ye may know that he is, by the power of the Holy Ghost; wherefore I would exhort you that ye deny not the power of God; for he worketh by power, according to the faith of the children of men, the same today and tomorrow, and forever.[12]

From the title page to its final pages, the purpose of the Book of Mormon is plainly affirmed, declaring that "Jesus is the Christ,"[13] and that declaration can only be understood and received by the power of the Holy Ghost.

God speaks to those who speak to Him as He has directed. During His mortal ministry and frequently since His infinite Atonement, the Savior has repeated His counsel and promise to "ask, and it shall be given unto you; seek, and ye shall find; knock, and it shall be opened unto you."[14] The importance of this specific instruction with promise from the Savior and His prophets in these latter days can be seen in the fact that it is repeated twice in the Book of Mormon,[15] thirteen times in the Doctrine and Covenants,[16] once in the Pearl of Great Price,[17] and four times in the New Testament.[18]

It had a great influence on the Prophet Joseph Smith at a young age, and prophets have testified that we can receive direction in our lives, too. In speaking to the youth of the Church, President Nelson taught:

Imagine! [Joseph Smith] was your age when he was inspired by the words of the Apostle James: "If any of you lack wisdom, let him

---

12. Moroni 10:3–7.
13. Book of Mormon Title Page; 2 Nephi 26:12; Moroni 7:44.
14. 3 Nephi 14:7
15. 3 Nephi 14:7; 27:28–29.
16. Doctrine and Covenants 4:7; 6:5; 11:5; 12:5; 14:5; 18:18; 42:56; 49:26; 66:9; 75:27; 88:63–65; 101:27; 132:40.
17. Moses 6:52.
18. Matthew 7:7; Luke 11:9; James 1:5–6; 1 John 5:14–15.

ask of God." . . . Take your questions directly to your Heavenly Father in prayer. Ask Him in the name of Jesus Christ to guide you. You can learn for yourself, right now at your age, how to receive personal revelation, and nothing will make a bigger difference in your life than that. I promise you . . . that wherever you are in the world, wherever you are on the covenant path, even if at this moment you are not centered on the path, I promise you that if you will sincerely and persistently do the spiritual work needed to develop the crucial, spiritual skill of learning how to hear the whisperings from the Holy Ghost, you will have all the direction you will ever need in your life. You will be given answers to your questions in the Lord's own way and in His own time.[19]

There are important and essential teachings and explanations which we must understand that enhance our comprehension of these marvelous promises. For example, Jacob taught that we must be pure in heart, look unto God with firmness of mind, and pray with exceeding faith.[20] The Savior taught that when we ask "in the Spirit," we ask "according to the will of God," and in those circumstances, "it is done even as [we ask]."[21] God's great promise to Nephi, son of Helaman, was that "all things shall be done unto thee according to thy word, for thou shalt not ask that which is contrary to my will."[22]

In His personal life and ministry, the Savior said and did only those things that the Father wanted Him to say and do.[23] He acknowledged the Father's responses, and in so doing provided an important lesson in the importance of our acknowledging that the Father also speaks to us. "And Jesus lifted up his eyes, and said, Father, I thank thee that thou hast heard me. And I knew that thou hearest me always: but because of the people which stand by I said it, that they may believe that thou hast sent me."[24]

As spirit children of a loving Heavenly Father, in the scriptures we can learn much from our eldest spirit brother, the Lord Jesus Christ, about recognizing the voice of the Father and having the courage to act in faith upon that which is communicated to us. Prayer is central to this divine means of communication. Once again, it is important to know and believe that

---

19. Russell M. Nelson, 2018 Worldwide Devotional for Youth, June 3, 2018.
20. Jacob 3:1.
21. Doctrine and Covenants 46:30.
22. Helaman 10:5.
23. John 4:34; 5:19; 6:38; 12:49–50.
24. John 11:41–42.

there is no substitute for prayer in our quest to receive the direction, peace, and comfort of the Spirit, to hear the voice of God. And in knowing and believing this, it is important that we joyfully practice it. There is power in knowing that the Savior of the world sought through prayer to know the will of His Father and the strength to follow it. There are numerous scriptural accounts of the Savior praying. We will consider five of them.

1. He prayed prior to calling the Twelve

> And it came to pass in those days, that he went out into a mountain to pray, and continued all night in prayer to God.
> And when it was day, he called unto him his disciples: and of them he chose twelve whom also he named apostles.[25]

During the days prior to the Savior going into the mountain to pray, He, on the Sabbath day, had restored whole the withered right hand of a man worshipping in the synagogue. Seeing this, the scribes and Pharisees had been "filled with madness; and communed one with another what they might do to Jesus."[26] In the midst of this unbelief, confusion, and opposition, with the important work of His Father before him the Savior separated himself into a mountain to pray—to commune with His Father in Heaven. As we think about their communication, we remember that the Father had given His Son "not the Spirit by measure, for he dwelleth in him, even the fullness."[27]

The scriptures do not say exactly what Jesus addressed with His Father in prayer, but the phrase "and when it was day" communicates that the work of the Father in calling the Twelve must have been a prominent part, for immediately following the prayer, without delay He called together His disciples and from among them He chose twelve.

In considering the Savior's example, it is helpful to remember that Matthew, Mark, Luke, John the Baptist, affirmed by John the Beloved, and Nephi all bore witness that the Holy Ghost descended from heaven and abode upon the Savior.[28] John the Baptist gave the following beautiful testimony as recorded in the Doctrine and Covenants.

---

25. Luke 6:12–13 (12–16).
26. Luke 6:6–11.
27. JST John 3:34.
28. Matthew 3:16–17; Mark 1:10–11; Luke 3:22; John 1:32; 1 Nephi 11:27; 2 Nephi 31:8.

And I, John, bear record, and lo, the heavens were opened, and the Holy Ghost descended upon him in the form of a dove, and sat upon him, and there came a voice out of heaven saying: This is my beloved Son.

And I, John, bear record that he received a fulness of the glory of the Father;

And he received all power, both in heaven and on earth, and the glory of the Father was with him, for he dwelt in him.[29]

This adds meaning to our understanding of the precious gift of the Holy Ghost that the Father has given to us.

In the midst of all the opposition and turmoil created by others around Him, the Savior continued to pray to His Father and received His Father's direction. And when it was received, He acted on it.

2. He prayed as He taught His disciples of His divine mission

And it came to pass, as he was alone praying, his disciples were with him: and he asked them, saying, Whom say the people that I am?[30]

While we are accustomed to appropriately thinking that all that the Savior did as the Son of God was of divine origin, it is worth noting that the Savior had been praying when He asked them one of the most inspired questions in all of scripture. This question elicited from His disciples careful thought and consideration, with informative responses. Ultimately, however, Peter made an inspired declaration of divine truth in the form of testimony: "The Christ of God."[31]

Realizing that "no man can say that Jesus is the Lord, but by the Holy Ghost,"[32] we see that through prayer and the operation of the Spirit, the Lord not only asked the appropriate question at the proper time, but Peter, and no doubt the others, were blessed through the ministration of the Spirit. It can be the same with all of us in our personal lives and in teaching one another, especially the rising generation, as we are blessed by the ministration of the Spirit and continue in that communion.

---

29. Doctrine and Covenants 93:15–17.
30. Luke 9:18.
31. Luke 9:20.
32. 1 Corinthians 12:3.

3. As He prayed, He taught His disciples to pray, helping them to know that answers would come by the Holy Spirit to them that ask

> And it came to pass, that, as he was praying in a certain place, when he ceased, one of his disciples said unto him, Lord, teach us to pray. . . .
>
> And he said unto them, Which of you shall have a friend, and shall go unto him at midnight, and say unto him, Friend, lend me three loaves. . . .
>
> And he from within shall answer and say . . . I cannot rise and give thee.
>
> . . . [Y]et because of his importunity he will rise and give him as many as he needeth.
>
> And I say unto you, Ask, and it shall be given you; seek, and ye shall find; knock, and it shall be opened unto you.
>
> For every one that asketh receiveth; and he that seeketh findeth; and to him that knocketh it shall be opened.
>
> If a son shall ask bread of any of you that is a father, will he give him a stone? . . .
>
> If ye then, being evil, know how to give good gifts unto your children: how much more shall your heavenly Father give the Holy Spirit to them that ask him?[33]

After many experiences of being with the Savior as He prayed, one of His disciples made a request that was perhaps in many hearts. Because of the Savior's example, His disciples wanted to know more about how to pray.

The Savior instructed them, providing a pattern for prayer. But perhaps sensing a possible lack of appreciation among His disciples for the fact that beyond the words of prayer, there is great significance in the relationship between the one asking and the One giving, Jesus taught them much more, drawing parallels from their everyday lives.

When a man in need asks of his friend assistance, because of time or circumstance, the friend may initially refuse him. But with the man's continual importuning, ultimately the friend who has the means will give to the man according to his need. Although the principle the Savior was teaching was evident in relationships between friends, He made it even clearer with a reference to their roles as fathers.

---

33. Luke 11:1–13.

The Savior then made a purposeful connection to what the Father will give: the Holy Spirit. In whatever manner the Savior taught the lesson, what the disciples felt and heard could have been something like the following:

> Beloved disciples, you have seen my example. I have given you a pattern in prayer and have helped you understand from your earthly experiences how willing your Heavenly Father is to give according to your requests. However, please don't miss the most important lesson: When you are in need, as I have been, ask the Father for the blessings of the ministry of the Holy Ghost, and He will give it.

What a blessing it is to see this present in our lives, as we learn to recognize and respond to the voice of the Lord.

4. He prayed for His chief apostle, knowing of the trials before him

> And the Lord said, Simon, Simon, behold, Satan hath desired to have you, that he may sift you as wheat:
> But I have prayed for thee, that thy faith fail not: and when thou art converted, strengthen thy brethren.[34]

The Savior, no doubt, knew Peter's heart, mind, and disposition. With that knowledge, and knowing the trials that awaited Peter, the Savior prayed for him, prayed in Peter's behalf, even before the trials were upon him. And letting Peter know of His prayers for him, the Savior tasked Peter to strengthen those in similar circumstances. This was inviting Peter to think beyond himself and to more fully see his role in helping others navigate troubled waters.

We can do the same. We know the hearts, minds, and dispositions of those close to us. And beyond praying for them, that their faith fail not, we do well to invite them to look beyond themselves and to more fully see their roles in helping others.

5. He prayed at the time of His greatest personal agony

> And he came out, and went, as he was wont, to the mount of Olives. . . .
> . . . and kneeled down, and prayed.
> Saying, Father, if thou be willing, remove this cup from me: nevertheless not my will, but thine, be done.

---

34. Luke 22:31–32.

And there appeared an angel . . . strengthening him.

And being in an agony he prayed more earnestly. . . .

And when he rose up from prayer, and was come to his disciples, he found them sleeping for sorrow.[35]

There is no experience involving prayer in all of scripture more applicable to our lives than this. As we love God and keep His commandments,[36] in our personal moments of greatest agony, the Savior has made a promise: "And I will pray the Father, and he shall give you another Comforter, that he may abide with you for ever; Even the Spirit of truth."[37]

Paul explained, "[Don't be unduly concerned about anything]; but in every thing by prayer and supplication with thanksgiving let your requests be made known unto God. And the peace of God, which passeth all understanding, shall keep your hearts and minds through Christ Jesus."[38]

Prayer. The gift of the Holy Ghost. Love of God. Obedience to His commandments. The Savior's promise. Paul's helpful explanation. We can know that in this life, whatever comes, we may find peace and strength in our moments of greatest agony.

Following the Savior's ascension into heaven, the Apostles continued in the pattern of prayer He had taught them.

With Judas' death, he having taken his own life, a new apostle was needed to complete the quorum of the Twelve.

And in those days, Peter stood up in the midst of the disciples, and said. . . .

. . . of these which have companied with us all the time that the Lord Jesus went in and out among us,

Beginning from the baptism of John, unto that same day that he was taken up from us, must one be ordained to be a witness with us of his resurrection.

And they appointed two, Joseph . . . and Matthias.

And they prayed, and said, Thou, Lord, which knows the hearts of all men, shew whether of these two thou hast chosen,

---

35. Luke 22:39–46.
36. John 14:15.
37. John 14:16–17.
38. Philippians 4:6–7, using language from the translation of the Greek as found in the footnote to verse 6 as found in the New Testament published by The Church of Jesus Christ of Latter-day Saints.

That he may take part of this ministry and apostleship, from which Judas by transgression fell. . . .

And they gave forth their lots; and the lot fell upon Matthias; and he was numbered with the eleven apostles.[39]

The Apostles continued to follow this same pattern of coming to know the will of the Lord through prayer when calling people to serve in the kingdom with the calling and setting apart of seven men to assist the Twelve in their duties,[40] in the calling of Paul and Barnabas,[41] and with Paul and Barnabas organizing local units of the church.[42]

The Savior had taught the Apostles that through the Holy Ghost, the Father would answer their questions and give comfort and direction. The Apostles now prayed for those in Samaria who had received the word of God, "that they might receive the Holy Ghost. Then laid they their hands on them, and they received the Holy Ghost."[43]

Among those prayers receiving answers that are of eternal significance and consequence for all mankind, companion to the Savior's prayer in the Garden of Gethsemane in the meridian of time, is the Prophet Joseph's prayer[44] opening this last dispensation, the dispensation of the fulness of times.[45] It was the prayer of a fourteen–year-old boy who prayed with real intent, having faith that he would receive an answer. According to Joseph, the prayer was prompted by the Lord's scriptural invitation and promise, "If any of you lack wisdom, let him ask of God, that giveth to all men liberally, and upbraideth not; and it shall be given him."[46]

This invitation and promise are to all of God's children, with the Prophet Joseph's affirmation that God will respond. But we must ask with real intent, having faith in Christ, believing that we will receive, willing to act in faith upon the communication that will come.

In learning to recognize and respond to the voice of the Spirit, there is no substitute for the scriptures, and there is no substitute for prayer.

---

39. Acts 1:15–26.
40. Acts 6:2–6.
41. Acts 13:1–4.
42. Acts 14:23.
43. Acts 8:14–17.
44. Joseph Smith—History 1:7–20.
45. Ephesians 1:10.
46. Joseph Smith—History 1:11. See also James 1:5.

10

FAITHFUL, MULTI-GENERATIONAL FAMILIES

Numerous scriptural references[1] to the Abrahamic covenant found in the four Standard Works of the Church[2] evidence the significance of the sacred promises associated with the covenant. Not surprisingly, of those many scriptural references, one found in the book of Abraham in the Pearl of Great Price provides the greatest detail as to the "who," the "what," and the "how" of the covenant.

> And I will make of thee a great nation, and I will bless thee above measure, and make thy name great among all nations, and thou shalt be a blessing unto thy seed after thee, that in their hands they shall bear this ministry and Priesthood unto all nations.
>
> And I will bless them through thy name; for as many as receive this Gospel shall be called after thy name, and shall be accounted thy seed, and shall rise up and bless thee, as their father;
>
> And I will bless them that bless thee, and curse them that curse thee; and in thee (that is, in thy Priesthood) and in thy seed (that is, thy Priesthood), for I give unto thee a promise that this right shall continue in thee, and in thy seed after thee (that is to say, the literal seed, or the seed of the

---

1. See, for example, Genesis 12:3; 18:18; 22:17–18; Acts 3:25; Galatians 3:7–9; 1 Nephi 15:18; 22:9; 3 Nephi 20:25; Doctrine and Covenants110:12; 124:58; Abraham 2:11.
2. The Holy Bible; the Book of Mormon—Another Testament of Jesus Christ; the Doctrine and Covenants; and the Pearl of Great Price.

body) shall all the families of the earth be blessed, even with the blessings
of the Gospel, which are the blessings of salvation, even of life eternal.[3]

Who? This is God covenanting with Abraham regarding all the families[4] of the earth. What? The covenant is that all the families of the earth will be blessed with the blessings of the gospel, which are the blessings of salvation, even of life eternal. How? By Abraham's righteous descendants and the Priesthood of God that they bear, the Melchizedek Priesthood, including the sealing power and authority.

The "when" is noted by Nephi in the Book of Mormon, "pointing to the covenant which should be fulfilled *in the latter days*; which covenant the Lord made to our father Abraham."[5]

And in the Book of Moses, God himself answers the "why." "For behold, this is my work and my glory—to bring to pass the immortality and eternal life of man."[6]

With the sealing of families for eternity, the realization of the core purpose of this covenant is evidenced through multi-generational families as each generation of the family faithfully lives the gospel of Jesus Christ and is blessed by His grace, being sealed together as families for time and for all eternity in God's temples, and faithfully passing the gospel on to each succeeding generation.

President Brigham Young recorded in his journal for Tuesday, February 23, 1847, a remarkable dream in which he received instructions from Joseph Smith, martyred nearly three years earlier. Brigham had asked to better understand "sealing principles." Joseph's response is particularly significant in connecting the blessing of life eternal with our capacity to hear and respond to the voice of the Spirit. This revelatory counsel from Joseph addresses the blessings that are the core of the Abrahamic covenant and are available only through the sealing of families together in the temples of God by the sealing authority conferred upon some bearers of the Melchizedek Priesthood.

> I said, "Brother Joseph, the brethren you know well, better than I do; you raised them up, and brought the Priesthood to us. The brethren

---

3. Abraham 2:9–11.
4. Besides "families," other scriptural references use "nations," "kindreds," and "generations."
5. 1 Nephi 15:18; emphasis added.
6. Moses 1:39.

have a great anxiety to understand the law of adoption or sealing principles; and if you have a word of counsel for me I should be glad to receive it."

Joseph stepped toward me, and looking very earnestly yet pleasantly said, "Tell the people to be humble and faithful, and be sure to keep the spirit of the Lord and it will lead them right. Be careful and not turn away the small still voice; it will teach you what to do and where to go; it will yield the fruits of the kingdom. Tell the brethren to keep their hearts open to conviction, so that when the Holy Ghost comes to them, their hearts will be ready to receive it. They can tell the Spirit of the Lord from all other spirits; it will whisper peace and joy to their souls; it will take malice, hatred, strife and all evil from their hearts; and their whole desire will be to do good, bring forth righteousness and build up the kingdom of God. Tell the brethren if they will follow the spirit of the Lord they will go right. Be sure to tell the people to keep the Spirit of the Lord; and if they will, they will find themselves just as they were organized by our Father in Heaven before they came into the world. Our Father in Heaven organized the human family, but they are all disorganized and in great confusion."

Joseph then showed me the pattern, how they were in the beginning. This I cannot describe, but I saw it, and saw where the Priesthood had been taken from the earth and how it must be joined together, so that there would be a perfect chain from Father Adam to his latest posterity. Joseph again said, "Tell the people to be sure to keep the Spirit of the Lord and follow it, and it will lead them just right."[7]

Remember, Brigham's question was about sealing principles. And Joseph responded by explaining that Heavenly Father desires to have the human family organized in a perfect chain from Father Adam to his latest posterity. This is the essence of the families of the earth being "blessed, even with the blessings of the gospel, which are the blessings of salvation, even of life eternal." In this vision, Joseph repeatedly emphasized to Brigham that if the Saints would "keep the Spirit of the Lord," that Spirit would lead them right. Joseph repeated: "Be sure to tell the people to keep the Spirit of the Lord; and if they will, they will find themselves just as they were organized by our Father in Heaven before they came into the world." Faithful multi-generational families are perpetuated when each

---

7. Elden J. Watson, *Manuscript History of Brigham Young, 1846–1847* (Sat Lake City: Privately printed, 1971).

person in each generation learns to recognize and respond to the voice of the Spirit, which leads them to the Savior and the crowning ordinances of His gospel, the sacred sealing ordinances of the temple.

As noted in Brigham's account, the prophet Joseph and Brigham were talking about the desire of "the brethren," and in a larger sense, the members of the Church. They were talking about those who had already covenanted with the Lord in the waters of baptism and had received the gift of the Holy Ghost. Accordingly, Joseph's counsel was to "keep" the Spirit of the Lord. His counsel is applicable to all in the Church. In summary, Joseph's counsel is this:

- Be humble and faithful.
- Be careful and do not turn away the small still voice.
    - It will teach you what to do and where to go.
    - It will yield the fruits of the kingdom.
- Keep your hearts open to conviction.
    - When the Holy Ghost comes to you, your hearts will be ready to receive it.
- You can tell the Spirit of the Lord from all other spirits.
    - It will whisper peace and joy to your souls.
    - It will take malice, hatred, strife, and all evil from your hearts.
    - Your whole desire will be to do good, bring forth righteousness, and build up the kingdom of God.

This is not a "hit or miss" proposition. It is always a "hit." Those who have received the gift of the Holy Ghost have received the right, promised by our Heavenly Father, to the constant companionship of the Holy Ghost, conditioned on faithfulness and obedience. We may do things that inhibit or prohibit our ability to hear that voice. But when we repent and follow the counsel Joseph gave to Brigham, the Spirit will "lead [us] just right."

Conversion is much more than compliance. While there are times when outward compliance may foster conversion, there are also times when outward compliance may temporarily mask an unbelieving heart. However, when a heart is fully converted, compliance becomes a manifestation of love.[8] The difference is always in the heart, for the heart is the venue

---

8. John 14:15.

of true conversion. As an example, this distinction can be seen in merely being present at sacrament meeting each Sunday with one's mind and heart elsewhere, or participating in sacrament meeting as an integral part of Sabbath day worship where we "offer up [our] sacraments upon [God's] holy day . . . rest[ing] from [our] labors . . . pay[ing] [our] devotions unto the Most High . . . [offering our vows] up in righteousness . . . offer[ing] [our] oblations and [our] sacraments unto the Most High . . . [and] confessing [our] sins . . . before the Lord."[9]

The source of conversion within the heart is the Spirit of the Lord. Therefore, in fostering faithful, converted multi-generational families, we must be careful not to misread outward compliance as inward conversion, and must be diligent in doing all possible to connect children and other loved ones with the Spirit of the Lord.

Again, the passing of faith and conversion from one generation to the next is not automatic. Conversion, which comes through the Spirit, is not some external thing that can be handed from one generation to the next. And while external things of powerful import such as the plates of Nephi, or the sword of Laban, or the Liahona, were passed from generation to generation, the focus among the prophets was first on the passing of faith and conversion.

In a September 2017 Worldwide Devotional for Young Adults, Elder David A. Bednar referenced an earlier teaching by President Gordon B. Hinckley to the students at BYU–Idaho in which he counseled them, "Do not become a weak link in your chain of generations." Elder Bednar then invited all of us to "become a welding link in the chain of generations."[10]

The Book of Mormon provides powerful lessons relating to faithful multi-generational families. For example, we regularly make reference to the familiar fact that the principal Book of Mormon record dealing with the prophet Lehi's family covers a period of approximately one thousand years, from about 600 BC to about 400 AD. What may not be as familiar to us is that over those one thousand years, the record was kept and preserved by four branches of Lehi's family involving eighteen generations, as outlined in the following chart. In identifying the four families below, we acknowledge that all keepers of this sacred record were understandably descendants of the prophet Lehi.

---

9. Doctrine and Covenants 59:9–12.
10. David A. Bednar, "A Welding Link," Worldwide Devotional for Young Adults, September 10, 2017, broadcast originating from the Apex North Carolina Stake Center.

As seen in the heading of the chart below, Lehi, of course, began the record. King Benjamin's father, Mosiah, was warned to "flee out of the land of Nephi,"[11] being one of "the children of Nephi."[12] Alma is identified by Mormon as "being a descendant of Nephi."[13] And Mormon identifies himself as being "a pure descendant of Lehi" and "a descendant of Nephi."[14] Nonetheless, because the Book of Mormon genealogical record is not compete in every detail, we identify the families as four different branches of Lehi's extended family. It is particularly noteworthy that with all of this, the record provides the name of each person in each generation principally responsible for keeping the record.

Book of Mormon — 18 Generations

Lehi's Family: 8 Generations
King Benjamin's Branch of the Family: Intermediaries
Alma's Branch of the Family: 8 Generations
Mormon's Branch of the Family: 2 Generations

GENERATION	NAME(S)	REFERENCES
1	Lehi	1 Nephi 1:5; Doctrine and Covenants 3: Heading
2	Nephi/Jacob	1 Nephi 1:1; 18:7; Jacob 1:1–2
3	Enos	Jacob 7:27
4	Jarom	Jarom 1:1
5	Omni	Jarom 1:15; Omni 1:1–2
6	Amaron/Chemish	Omni 1:3, 8

---

11. Omni 1:12.
12. Mosiah 11:13.
13. Mosiah 17:2.
14. 3 Nephi 5:20; Mormon 1:5

7	Abinadom	Omni 1:10
8	Amaleki/King Benjamin	Omni 1:12
	Amaleki to King Benjamin King Benjamin to Mosiah Mosiah to Alma the Younger	Omni 1:25 Mosiah 28:11 Mosiah 28:20
9	Mosiah/Alma	Mosiah 26:8
10	Alma the Younger	Mosiah 28:20
11	Helaman/Shiblon	Alma 37:1–2; 45:2, 9; 50:38; 63:1
12	Helaman son of Helaman	Helaman— Heading
13	Nephi	Helaman— Heading
14	Nephi son of Nephi	3 Nephi 1:2
15	Amos	4 Nephi 1:19
16	Amos son of Amos/ Ammaron	4 Nephi 1:21, 47–49
17	Mormon	Mormon 1:1
18	Moroni	Words of Mormon 1:1; Mormon 8:1, 12–14; Moroni 10:1–2

Although it was Nephi who kept the record in the first part of the Book of Mormon as it has come to us, the record translated by Joseph Smith began with the book of Lehi, which comprised the 116 pages that were lost by Martin Harris. We therefore begin with Lehi in showing that Lehi's relationship-identifiable family was responsible for the record for eight generations, from Lehi to Amaleki. After receiving the record from Amaleki, king Benjamin's branch of the family effectively served as an intermediary in keeping, preserving, and then transferring the record to Alma's branch of the family over one generation. As seen above, king Benjamin's son, Mosiah, and Alma the Elder were of the same generation, and Mosiah had given Alma "authority over the church," which must have included some responsibility for the sacred record. Indeed, it was Alma who recorded the words of Abinadi[15] and provided "the account of Alma and his brethren."[16] However, after just one generation, Mosiah delivered the record to Alma's son, Alma the Younger. Understanding that Alma the Elder at least shared some responsibility for the record with Mosiah, we begin with Alma the Elder and we see that his branch of the family was then responsible for the record for eight generations to Ammaron. Ammaron then delivered the record to next-generation Mormon, who finally delivered it to his son, Moroni, thus covering the final two generations.

Now, apart from the detail of these specific names, consider deeply the significance of the teaching, counseling, letter writing, nurturing, admonishing, and love being passed from one generation to the next that allowed for these eighteen generations of faithful sons to bring forth the miraculous work, the Book of Mormon. True it is that not every generation was perfect. Omni declares, "I of myself am a wicked man, and I have not kept the statutes and the commandments of the Lord as I ought to have done."[17] But even in that confession is the testimony of the statutes and commandments of the Lord. And somehow, his two sons, Amaron and Chemish, were righteous and faithful. They didn't leave the fold. We can see in this a testament to their faithful mothers. Indeed, the work and evidence of faithful mothers are found in every generation.

Apart from the Omni experience, consider the overwhelming evidence of the value in the passing of faith in the Lord Jesus Christ and the confidence in recognizing and responding to the voice of the Spirit from one generation to the next. The examples fill the Book of Mormon. Just to mention a few, Nephi saw his father, Lehi, speak "with power, being filled with the Spirit."[18] Lehi implored his son, Jacob, to "choose eternal life, according to the will of [the great Mediator's] Holy Spirit; and not choose

---

15. Mosiah 17:4.
16. Mosiah 25:6.
17. Omni 1:2.
18. 1 Nephi 2:14.

eternal death, according to the will of the flesh."[19] Enos, Jacob's son, proclaimed his father "a just man—for he taught me in . . . the nurture and admonition of the Lord."[20] And how does one know the nurture and admonition of the Lord without knowing the voice of the Lord? Jarom, son of Omni, taught, "There are many among us who have many revelations . . . and . . . have communion with the Holy Spirit, which maketh manifest unto the children of men according to their faith."[21]

As taught by an angel, King Benjamin taught Mosiah, his other sons, and all of us, this powerful truth: "The natural man is an enemy to God, and has been from the fall of Adam, and will be forever and ever, unless he yields to the enticings of the Holy Spirit, and putteth off the natural man."[22]

Mosiah and Alma certainly had challenges with their children, but they continued to pray in faith for the sons of Mosiah and Alma the Younger. Eventually, their wayward sons were visited by an angel, but it says much for the teachings of Mosiah and Alma the Elder that after the angel's visit, their sons attributed their conversion and communion with the Spirit to fasting and prayer. Said Alma the Younger,

> I do know that these things whereof I have spoken are true. And how do ye suppose that I know of their surety?
>
> Behold, . . . they are made known unto me by the Holy Spirit of God. Behold, I have fasted and prayed many days that I might know these things of myself. And now I do know of myself that they are true; for the Lord God hath made them manifest unto me by his Holy Spirit.[23]

Mormon said of the sons of Mosiah, "They had given themselves to much prayer, and fasting; therefore they had the spirit of prophecy, and the spirit of revelation."[24] These same truths and testimonies are found throughout the Book of Mormon.

At the beginning of this book, I told of a letter my father wrote to me not long after the beginning of my calling to serve as a full-time missionary for the Church in which he communicated to me the

---

19. 2 Nephi 2:28–29.
20. Enos 1:1.
21. Jarom 1:4.
22. Mosiah 3:19.
23. Alma 5:45–46.
24. Alma 17:3.

importance of recognizing and following the voice of Spirit and shared with me his personal testimony. On this occasion, he was responding to my question on a personal matter. There is an account in the Book of Mormon of another father giving counsel to his son, in this instance on a doctrinal matter, again, not long after the son's calling to the ministry. While the topic was the error of baptizing little children, like my father, Mormon made clear that the answer is found not in man's wisdom but in prayer to the Lord and the ministration of the Spirit. Wrote Mormon to Moroni, "For immediately after I had learned these things of you I inquired of the Lord concerning the matter. And the word of the Lord came to me by the power of the Holy Ghost."[25]

Such timely and inspired communications from parents to children are powerfully influential in the lives of children. The same is true with our timely and inspired communications with all of those we know and love.

Central to the initiation and perpetuation of faithful multi-generational families fully converted to the gospel of Jesus Christ is the capacity of individuals in each generation to recognize and respond to the voice of the Spirit. Like the parents in the faithful multi-generational families in the Book of Mormon, parents and trusted adults today must do everything possible to connect all within the family to the Spirit. In so doing, the covenant God made with Abraham is fulfilled, the purposes of God are realized, and His name is glorified.

---

25. Moroni 8:7.

11

DOCTRINE

YEARS AGO, I WAS INTRIGUED BY THE different phrases in scripture used to describe our journey in learning to recognize and respond to the voice of the Spirit. Earlier in this book[1] we learned of the significance of what it meant for Nephi and Lehi, the sons of Helaman, to "grow up unto the Lord" in times of great turmoil, and the peace and confidence that came to them, because of their ability to hear and respond to the voice of the Spirit.

The Kirtland Temple dedicatory prayer was given to the Prophet Joseph Smith by revelation and directly connects growing up unto the Lord with receiving a fulness of the Holy Ghost, thereby being prepared to receive every needful thing. Consider the significance of these words: "And that they may grow up in thee, and receive a fulness of the Holy Ghost, and be organized according to thy laws, and be prepared to obtain every needful thing."[2]

Beyond Mormon's description of what he observed in the lives of Nephi and Lehi that evidenced their growing up unto the Lord, under the inspiration of heaven, Joseph here prayed that all of us, all of God's children, would grow up unto Him. And that growing up would be evidenced by receiving a fullness of the Holy Ghost. This is a direct statement of our Heavenly Father's intent. He earnestly desires that we obtain every needful thing throughout our earthly sojourn. And the means He has provided to do so is the precious gift of the Holy Ghost.

---

1. See chapter 2, "Peace in Times of Turmoil."
2. Doctrine and Covenants 109:15.

Also earlier in this book, we learned how central being "sober" and "quick to observe," this sensitivity to spiritual direction, was in Mormon's marvelous ministry wherein he was called to abridge the Nephite record as an entire nation dwindled in unbelief.

We have been admonished to help others "understand the doctrine of repentance, faith in Christ the Son of the living God, and of baptism and the gift of the holy Ghost by the laying on of the hands . . . and . . . to pray, and to walk uprightly before the Lord."[3] Understanding the doctrine of the gift of the Holy Ghost by the laying on of hands of necessity involves more than merely understanding hands physically being placed on heads and words invoking the authority of the Melchizedek priesthood. In addition to these essentials, understanding the doctrine involves knowing and experiencing that this is the means by which God communicates with His faithful sons and daughters and that it is real. Additional examples bring added insights.

The Light of Christ, the power of the Holy Ghost, and the gift of the Holy Ghost

Before considering other phrases, an understanding of three principal means of divine spiritual communication is helpful in comprehending how the Lord speaks to us and how we hear Him: the Light of Christ, the power of the Holy Ghost, and the gift of the Holy Ghost.

The Spirit of Christ or the Light of Christ is given to every mortal being and is the means by which all are able to judge between good and evil.[4] It "is just what the words imply: enlightenment, knowledge, and an uplifting, ennobling, persevering influence that comes upon mankind because of Jesus Christ." It is not "the personage of the Holy Ghost, for the light of Christ is not a personage at all."[5]

The power of the Holy Ghost is the means by which the Holy Ghost, a personage of spirit and the third member of the Godhead, communicates and bears witness of "the truth of all things."[6] This power is distinct from the gift of the Holy Ghost and can be felt by those who have not yet received the gift of the Holy Ghost. However, although one may feel the

3. Doctrine and Covenants 68:25–28; see also Moses 6:57–61.
4. Moroni 7:16–19.
5. LDS Bible Dictionary, "Light of Christ."
6. Moroni 10:5.

power of the Holy Ghost, without having received the gift of the Holy Ghost, that person has no promise of the power or influence of the Holy Ghost remaining with him.

"The gift [of the Holy Ghost] can come only after proper and authorized baptism and is conferred by the laying on of hands. . . . . [It] is the right to have, whenever one is worthy, the [constant] companionship of the Holy Ghost."[7] Concerning this gift, President Wilford Woodruff taught,

> I can say unto you that there is no greater gift, there is no greater blessing, there is no greater testimony given to any man on earth. You may have the administration of angels; you may see many miracles; you may see many wonders in the earth; but I claim that the gift of the Holy Ghost is the greatest gift that can be bestowed upon man.[8]

President Woodruff also taught the following:

> Every man or woman that has ever entered into the church of God and been baptized for the remission of sins has a right to revelation, a right to the Spirit of God, to assist them in their labors, in their administrations to their children, in counseling their children and those over whom they are called upon to preside. The Holy Ghost is not restricted to men, nor to apostles or prophets; it belongs to every faithful man and woman, and to every child who is old enough to receive the gospel of Christ.[9]

In the April 2018 general conference of the Church, President Russell M. Nelson taught powerfully concerning revelation and the role of the Holy Ghost:

> The privilege of receiving revelation is one of the greatest gifts of God to His children. . . .
> If we will truly receive the Holy Ghost and learn to discern and understand His promptings, we will be guided in matters large and small. . . .
> Pray in the name of Jesus Christ about your concerns, your fears, your weaknesses—yes, the very longings of your heart. And then listen! Write the thoughts that come to your mind. Record your feelings and follow through with actions that you are prompted to take. As you

7. LDS Bible Dictionary, "Holy Ghost."
8. *Teachings of Presidents of the Church: Wilford Woodruff*, Chapter 5, "The Holy Ghost and Personal Revelation," 49. *Deseret Weekly*, April 6, 1889, 451.
9. Ibid; *The Discourses of Wilford Woodruff*, 53.

repeat this process day after day, month after month, year after year, you will "grow into the principle of revelation." (*Teaching of Presidents of the Church: Joseph Smith*, 132.)

Our Savior and Redeemer, Jesus Christ, will perform some of His mightiest works between now and when He comes again. . . . But in coming days, it will not be possible to survive spiritually without the guiding, directing, comforting, and constant influence of the Holy Ghost.[10]

Understanding these three principle means of divine spiritual communication can help us focus more particularly on how we recognize and respond to the influence of the Holy Ghost.

Taught in all the ways of God

The great prophet Enoch declared simply, "And my father taught me in all the ways of God."[11] That is a marvelous tribute to his father! Being taught in all the ways of God encompasses many things. Among them, we find this defining characteristic: "And it came to pass that Enoch journeyed in the land, among the people; and as he journeyed, the Spirit of God descended out of heaven, and abode upon him."[12]

Indeed, the Lord told Enoch:

Go forth and do as I have commanded thee, and no man shall pierce thee. Open thy mouth, and it shall be filled, and I will give thee utterance, for all flesh is in my hands, and I will do as seemeth me good.

Say unto this people: Choose ye this day, to serve the Lord God who made you.

Behold, my Spirit is upon you, wherefore all thy words will I justify; and the mountains shall flee before you, and the rivers shall turn from their course; and thou shalt abide in me, and I in you; therefore walk with me.[13] And Enoch did walk with God.[14]

"My Spirit is upon you." "All thy words will I justify." "Thou shalt abide in me, and I in you." All these things involve the influence and

10. Russell M. Nelson, "Revelation for the Church, Revelation for Our Lives," April 2018 general conference, Sunday morning session.
11. Moses 6:41; see also Moses 6:21.
12. Moses 6:26.
13. Moses 6:32–34.
14. Moses 6:39.

workings of the Holy Ghost and were an important part of what Jared taught Enoch. While we see scriptural truths and doctrinal verities exemplified in Enoch's subsequent teachings, central to being taught in all the ways of God was Enoch's acquired ability to recognize and respond to God's voice, the voice of the Spirit. This was taught to him by his father. It was not merely teaching a knowledge or awareness of points of doctrine or familiarity with historical events and facts, although these are also important. However, the ways of God are founded in the truth that He does the teaching.[15] And He does the teaching through the precious gift of the Holy Ghost. Whatever else Jared taught Enoch, he taught him that.

Along with other things, written in the book of Enoch was the fact that Enoch was twenty-five years old when he was ordained under the hand of Adam; and he was sixty-five when Adam blessed him."[16] Knowing of that personal association with Adam provides added significance to Enoch teaching the people of the fall of Adam. Imagine being taught the fall of Adam by Adam! After rehearsing the consequence of the Fall, Enoch made known that God had made known unto their fathers that all men must repent and turn unto Him, and "hearken unto [His] voice," obeying the ordinances, declaring Jesus Christ "the only name which shall be given under heaven whereby salvation shall come unto the children of men," and then promising, "ye shall receive the gift of the Holy Ghost."[17]

We learn much more about what it meant for Enoch to be taught in all the ways of God from the Joseph Smith Translation of Genesis 14. Please give this careful attention and consideration.

In the sixteen verses (verses 25 though 40) that the Lord restored to Genesis 14 through the Prophet Joseph, we learn about Melchizedek and Abraham, but we learn about them through powerful references to Enoch, this great prophet who had been taught in all the ways of God.

Melchizedek "was ordained an high priest after the order of the covenant which God made with Enoch, [i]t being after the order of the Son of God."[18] Now read carefully the following verses:

> For God having sworn unto Enoch and unto his seed with an oath
> by himself; that every one being ordained after this order and calling

---

15. Doctrine and Covenants 43:16; 84:48.
16. Doctrine and Covenants 107:48–57.
17. Moses 6:47–52.
18. JST Genesis 14:27–28.

should have power, by faith, to break mountains, to divide the seas, to dry up waters, to turn them out of their course;

To put at defiance the armies of nations, to divide the earth, to break every band, to stand in the presence of God; to do all things according to his will, according to his command, subdue principalities and power; and this by the will of the Son of God which was from before the foundation of the world.[19]

This is an eternal truth. God has sworn unto Enoch and his seed with an oath, by himself, that everyone being ordained after the order of the Son of God, in other words, everyone worthily receiving the Melchizedek priesthood, shall have power, by faith, to move mountains and other mighty things.

But there is an essential, unequivocal qualifier. Do we see it? Do all the sons and daughters of God see it? That qualifier is "to do all things according to his will, according to his command . . . and this by the will of the Son of God."

Yes! There is mighty, heavenly power in the Melchizedek Priesthood. But that power is wholly conditioned upon righteous Melchizedek Priesthood bearers exercising faith in knowing and doing the will of the Son of God. And how will priesthood bearers know the will of the Son of God if they cannot hear His voice, the voice of the Spirit, to receive that will? And how will the will of the Son be done if the priesthood bearers lack the conviction to act when the direction is given?

Enoch was taught by his father in all the ways of God. Central to that was Enoch being taught how to recognize the voice of the Spirit and being imbued with the conviction to follow that voice.

Through Enoch the Lord affirmed the following: "Therefore it is given to abide in you; the record of heaven; the Comforter; the peaceable things of immortal glory; the truth of all things; that which quickeneth all things, which maketh alive all things; that which knoweth all things, and hath all power according to wisdom, mercy, truth, justice, and judgment."[20]

The Lord has given this to abide in all of His children. We have a sacred obligation to feel and follow it.

---

19. JST Genesis 14: 30–31.
20. Moses 6:61.

Nurture and admonition of the Lord

Enos described his father, Jacob, as a just man, not only because he had taught him in his language, but also because Jacob had taught him "in the nurture and admonition of the Lord."[21] Given Enos' experience that he recorded in hearing the voice of the Lord, more fully understanding the nurture and the admonition of the Lord will assist us in hearing the Lord's voice.

In the English language, we understand "nurture" to encompass a combined sense of nourishing, protecting, strengthening, and loving. Indeed, nurture is defined as "to care for and encourage the growth and development of."[22] But like other English words, it is difficult to translate "nurture" into other languages, which often requires using other descriptive words that may change according to context. [23] In the book of Enos, "nurture" and "admonition" are the English words the Lord gave to Joseph Smith to communicate what Enos had recorded in the language of his day.

In New Testament times, Paul provided counsel to all fathers using similar language: "And, ye fathers, provoke not your children to wrath: but bring them up in the nurture and admonition of the Lord."[24]

I am not a linguist, but my rudimentary search informs me that in this scripture, "paideia" is the Greek word translated into English as "nurture." The Greek meaning of paideia also seems to communicate "education" and "discipline" related to education. However, in Latin-based languages, paideia is translated to the English equivalent of "discipline," "doctrine," and "correction" to communicate Paul's meaning. In English, the first definition of discipline suggests the practice of training to obey rules with punishment as a consequence of disobedience. However, the second English meaning suggests a branch of knowledge studied in

---

21. Enos 1:1.
22. google.com/search?q=definition+of+nurture&rlz=1C5CHFA_enU-S703US810&oq=definition+of+nurture&aqs=chrome..69i57j0l5.7199j1j9&sourceid=chrome&ie=UTF-8
23. In the language of the gospel, "minister" is another English word requiring different words in various language translations to accurately convey meaning and understanding according to context.
24. Ephesians 6:4.

higher education.[25] The first and second meanings of discipline in the Latin-based languages are similar to those in English.

"Admonish" means to "warn or reprimand someone firmly."[26] Translations for English and for Latin-based languages uniformly use a form of admonition for both Paul's and Enos's references.

Perhaps Paul intended to communicate that fathers were to train their children to obey, with punishment as a consequence of disobedience, and with a reprimand. This interpretation would suggest he used discipline and admonition as dual expressions of the same concept. However, perhaps Paul intended to communicate two diverse but complimentary concepts of heavenly intervention. The first being divine learning and the second being divine warning.

Nevertheless, reading "nurture" in the English translation of Paul's counsel to fathers does not cause English speakers to think either in terms of training to obey with consequential punishment or in terms of higher education. Rather, it suggests personal, informed, loving interventions to strengthen and build.

Knowing that the prophet Joseph was not translating a Greek record, and having no basis for analyzing the language of Enos's day, we read "nurture" in English and understand, perhaps, a combined meaning of divine education that is nourishing, protecting, strengthening, and loving.

Those who have translated the "nourish" in the book of Enos from English into other Latin-based languages have generally used "discipline" or "correction" as used by those who translated Paul's words from Greek. (Portuguese uses "precepts.") One would need to look to the second meaning of discipline in those languages to understand what I am suggesting here for English.

As an example for understanding the meaning of nurture, consider the language found in "The Family: A Proclamation to the World." In the seventh paragraph we read, "Mothers are primarily responsible for the nurture

---

25. google.com/search?q=definition+of+disciplne&rlz=1C5CHFA_enUS703US810&oq=definition+of+disciplne&aqs=chrome..69i57j0l5.9175j1j7&sourceid=chrome&ie=UTF-8, accessed December 28, 2018.

26. google.com/search?rlz=1C5CHFA_enUS703US810&ei=ToMmXLWjBMi-50PEPsYCFoA8&q=definition+of+admonish&oq=definition+of+admonish&gs_l=psy-ab.3..0l2j0i22i30j0i22i10i30j0i22i30l6.14675.17263..18050...0.0..0.113.658.0j6......0....1..gws-wiz.......0i71j35i39j0i20i263.HSbj5D71VjA

of their children."[27] Generally speaking, we would understand this to mean that mothers are primarily responsible to care for and encourage the growth and development of their children, which would involve personal, informed, loving interventions that strengthen and build them. The Italian translation of this phrase uses the word "educare" and would suggest education beyond secular learning. Spanish uses "cuidado," meaning to look after, care for, and give attention to. Similarly, Portuguese uses "cuidar." French uses "élever," meaning to raise or to rear. I believe that the meaning of nurture communicated by the latter-day prophets in the Proclamation and as translated in other languages more closely aligns with the meaning intended by Enos when he spoke of his father's influence in his life.

"The nurture and admonition of the Lord." Through Jacob's example and teaching, Enos was not only taught two aspects of the Lord's interactions with His children, nurture and admonition, but he also experienced them, thus gaining his own personal testimony. God nurtures His children. Through interventions suited for each individual's needs He nourishes, protects, strengthens, and loves. In a perfect way He cares for those who are willing and obedient, and encourages their growth and development. God also admonishes His children. He warns and chastens firmly, including those who are willing and obedient, to keep them in the right way. And in large measure, He does all of this through the teachings of prophets and of other faithful church leaders and the timely interventions of loving family members.

God's nurturing and admonishing serve to provide the means for His children to come to recognize and respond to His voice.

The scriptures and the teachings of the prophets are replete with God's counsel to "[take] the Holy Spirit for [our] guide."[28] And gratefully, the Lord has provided many examples of those who have done so, providing insights and understanding as to how they honed this marvelous capacity. We have focused on just a few.

In His preface to the Doctrine and Covenants, the Lord said:

> Hearken, O ye people of my church . . . Hearken ye people from afar . . . listen together. . . .
>
> . . . The voice of the Lord is unto the ends of the earth, that all that will hear may hear . . . .

---

27. "The Family: A Proclamation to the World."
28. Doctrine and Covenants 45:57.

. . . but every man walketh in his own way, and after the image of his own god . . . .

Wherefore, I the Lord, knowing the calamity which should come upon the inhabitants of the earth called upon my servant Joseph Smith, Jun., and spake unto him from heaven, and gave him commandments . . . .

. . . That every man [and woman] might speak in the name of God the Lord, even the Savior of the world;

That faith also might increase in the earth.[29]

What a glorious insight! Our Heavenly Father speaks to all who will hear Him. He desires that we recognize His voice and follow Him rather than walking in our own way. He therefore provides direction through His prophets, to the end that His every son and every daughter may, with the gift of the Holy Ghost, speak in the name of the Savior in accomplishing His purposes with an increase in faith.

How blessed we are to live in this day!

29. Doctrine and Covenants 1:1, 11, 16, 17, 20–21.

12

PRACTICAL EXPERIENCE

AN EXPERIENCE AS A YOUNG MAN FOLLOWING high school graduation may provide an example from my life that seems to encapsulate several of the principles addressed in this book.

After high school I went to the University of Arizona in Tucson, Arizona, where I played basketball on the freshman team. Over fifty years ago, major four-year universities had freshman and varsity basketball teams, and only sophomores, juniors, and seniors played on the varsity teams. The freshman teams competed against other freshman teams and against junior college teams. Tucson was about a two-hour drive southeast of my home in Mesa. This was the first time I lived for an extended period away from home.

I had been taught the gospel by loving parents and had enjoyed the blessings of spiritual communications and affirmations. Accordingly, I had developed a private religious practice of regular scripture study and prayer, and Sunday worship in the "house of prayer."[1] However, I now found myself living among students, many of whom did not share the same values. Alcohol and promiscuity could be easily found by those who sought them. Some of my team members, all below the age of twenty-one and also away from their homes for the first time, secretly engaged in these things, even though team rules also prohibited them. I would not participate, and while we remained friends, our social paths soon began to diverge.

---

1. Doctrine and Covenants 59:9.

I lived in a dormitory with some of the other new athletes at the school. Fraternities and sororities were popular at the school, and among the students receiving attention to join were athletes. Indeed, athletes seemed to receive added attention. While I suppose some of them could have been fine organizations, I personally never felt comfortable in considering membership.

On one occasion, one of my teammates who was considering joining a particular fraternity, mostly to be able to move out of the dormitory and into the "frat house," invited me to get a date and go with him and his date to a fraternity party in the desert just outside of Tucson. I felt uncomfortable with this invitation but suppressed that feeling in the interest of fostering a closer friendship. I told him I might consider it, but that I didn't know a girl to invite on the date. He said that was not a problem and that he could arrange a date for me. I reminded him that I didn't smoke or drink and that I didn't want a date that did those things. He assured me that would not be a problem. With lingering suppressed feelings warning me against going, I clearly explained that I didn't want to attend a beer-drinking party, and that because it was Saturday night, I wanted to be back in the dormitory by midnight. Again he assured me that none of this would be a problem. With this, I told him I would go.

On Saturday night he picked me up in his vehicle with his date and mine. Both girls seemed to be pleasant young women, and we had a nice conversation as we drove out into the desert. When we arrived at the remote location, I saw that many vehicles were parked in a circular pattern around a large fire. And to my disappointment, I saw that there were several large kegs of beer in the circle, and everyone was drinking. We all got out of the car and my teammate and the girls all invited me to go with them and get some beer to drink. I asked my teammate why he had done this, and he replied that I was a college student now, away from home, and it was time for me to grow up and to stop being a kid. The girls joined in this, telling me I was a big boy now and I could prove it to them by drinking.

As upset as I was with my teammate, I was absolutely furious with myself. I could not believe I had quenched the Spirit and was now finding myself subject to worldly pressure to conform. Gratefully, I felt strengthened by the Spirit as I told them I would not participate in any way with them, that I would remain at the car the entire night, and that I would be anxious to leave as soon as possible. They laughed at me, turned, and went to get their drinks, convinced that I would eventually change my mind and join them.

Darkness soon came as the sun went down. I sat alone for a couple of hours, listening to the distant laughter and chatter, disappointed in myself for having put myself in such an unwanted position.

Perhaps around 11:00 p.m., I noticed the headlights of several vehicles coming across the desert to our location. Upon arriving in the area, the vehicles separated and formed a broad circle around all the other vehicles. Then, when they were all in place, evidently with a signal, red lights began flashing on the tops of the vehicles. They were police cars, and the police were raiding the party, doing an underage alcohol drinking bust. Some of the party participants began running into the desert. The police rounded most of them up. The police then set up a table with alcohol testing equipment, lined everyone up, told them to get out their identification, and began processing everyone to determine those underage who had been drinking. I was caught with the group, presumed to have been drinking. When they finally got to me, the policeman, with his head down and writing, began asking me the standard questions. I got his attention, looked him squarely in the eyes, and said something like the following: "I have not drunk any alcohol tonight. In fact I have never drunk alcohol in my life." The officer replied, "Yeah, I've been hearing that a lot tonight." I continued to look him directly in the eyes and said again, "You can believe me. I have been separate from this group the entire night, and I have had no alcohol." The officer looked at me for another moment, tilted his head a bit to one side, and said, "I believe you. You don't have to take the test." He asked how I had come to the party. I identified my teammate. The officer said my teammate would be detained and that he was in no condition to drive his car home. With my teammate's concurrence, the officer had me take the car keys and told me to leave.

As I recall, I arrived back at the dormitory around 2:00 Sunday morning. I was still upset with myself but was profoundly grateful that the officer had believed me, even though testing would have confirmed the absence of alcohol in my system. I readied for bed and finally went to sleep.

A preset alarm sounded at 6:45 a.m. I quickly turned it off. These were in the days prior to a single block of time for church meetings on Sunday. Priesthood meeting began at 7:00 a.m., followed by Sunday School and sacrament meeting, both held separately later on Sunday morning and Sunday evening. I was alone, away from home. It had been a short night. The thought came to me, "Just roll over and go back to sleep. No one will ever know." But that thought felt uncomfortable, and I felt a spiritual impression come into my heart and mind that said, "Get up and go to priesthood meeting." Not wanting to again quench the Spirit, I arose, quickly dressed, and walked to the chapel several minutes from the dormitory.

Opening exercises for priesthood meeting had already begun when I walked into the back of the chapel. As I started to walk up the aisle to find a seat, I immediately recognized the back of one of the heads in the congregation. It was my father. I quietly went up to the row where he was seated, slipped in, and sat down beside him. What next transpired I will never forget. He reached over with his hand, patted me a couple of times on the knee, and whispered, "I knew I would find you here, Son."

I am not able to adequately express the peace and joy I felt as I heard those words from my dearly loved earthly father, for as he spoke, I also heard in my heart and mind the voice of my Heavenly Father saying, "Yes. I knew I would find you here, Son."

Our ability to recognize and respond to the voice of the Spirit grows throughout our lives as we righteously exercise our agency. Our Heavenly Father is not a silent or a reluctant Parent. Because He loves us and wants us to become like Him, He has given to us His plan of happiness and has provided the means of communication through the voice of the Spirit which, when followed in faith through our righteous exercise of agency, is central to becoming like Him. This was perfectly exemplified in the life of His Only Begotten Son in the flesh when the Savior said, "I do nothing of myself; but as my Father hath taught me, I speak these things. And he that sent me is with me: the Father hath not left me alone; for I do always those things that please him."[2]

Our Father will not leave us alone. He wants to communicate with us. But He does not force us to listen. He speaks to us in our hearts and minds, and like an earthly father teaching his child to ride a bicycle, He knows we may occasionally fail. As we grow, in our daily experiences we gain confidence in our ability to recognize His voice and respond appropriately.

At times we may quench the Spirit, just as I did when agreeing to

2. John 8:28–29.

attend the party with my teammate. But our Heavenly Father doesn't give up on us, and when we recognize we have erred and attempt to make things right, He sustains our righteous efforts and continues to speak. This is all made possible because of our Savior's infinite Atonement. If, however, we repeatedly ignore God's voice, He awaits a time when we will be more receptive.

If we succumb to Satan's relentless pressure to conform to worldly standards, especially at a time when by divine design we are seeking our spiritual independence, our Father will let us know in our hearts and minds that we have erred. He will not force us to repent, but when we do, His approving communications are generous to overflowing. Why? Because He wants us to grow from our experience, learn to more clearly discern His voice, and draw closer to Him, becoming more like Him.

"Father hath not left [us] alone." And as the Lord taught through Amulek, "In the hearts of the righteous doth he dwell . . . and . . . the righteous shall sit down in his kingdom, to go no more out."[3] In that coming day, having grown up unto the Lord and having learned throughout our lives to follow His voice, and finding ourselves in His presence, we will feel His approving touch, and hear His affirming words, "Well done, Son, or Daughter. I knew I would find you here."

---

3. Alma 34:36.

ABOUT THE AUTHOR

CRAIG ALLEN CARDON WAS SUSTAINED AS A General Authority Seventy of The Church of Jesus Christ of Latter-day Saints in 2006. He served as a member of the Africa West Area presidency, an assistant executive director in the Priesthood and Family Department, the editor of Church magazines, and a member of the Pacific Area presidency. He became an Emeritus General Authority in 2018.

He chaired committees in the Priesthood and Family Department that, under the direction of the Twelve Apostles, developed the new "Come, Follow Me" church curriculum and the new children and youth initiatives.

He married Deborah L. Dana in 1970. They are the parents of eight children. As of 2020, they have forty-six grandchildren and three great-grandchildren.